UNIVERSAL WISDOM FOR MODERN TIMES

UNIVERSAL WISDOM FOR MODERN TIMES

A. M. HALLIDAY

First Edition 2017

69 Highlever Road,
London W10 6PR

www.hpstrust.org.uk

ISBN 978-0-9956971-0-2

Printed and bound by
CPI Group (UK) Ltd, Croydon, CR0 4YY

FOREWORD

Dr Anthony Martin Halliday (1926–2008) was a man whose talents were as varied as they were exceptional. Whilst he carried out internationally acclaimed pioneering work in the field of electroencephalography at the National Hospital for Neurology and Neurosurgery at Queen Square, London for almost 40 years, he also acquired a deep understanding of Adhyatma Yoga (the Yoga of Self-Knowledge) under the direct instruction of a traditional teacher, Dr Hari Prasad Shastri

He understood 'science' both through the practical reality of his day-to-day work and also philosophically through energetic study. Both science and this Yoga being an enquiry into truth, he found that when properly understood, science does not contradict or conflict with the 'spiritual' and universal views of Adhyatma Yoga – indeed, it is notable that he often supported his teachings with quotes from many eminent scientists and held their unselfish pursuit of truth, in very high regard.

This selection of thirteen public lectures, given between 1961 and 1977, shows that many western thinkers have come to the same conclusions as those imparted in the universal teachings of Adhyatma Yoga. Dr Halliday produces not only a strong argument for the timeless veracity of these ancient teachings from this finding, but also the relevance of implementing them practically in daily life.

If taken together they should stimulate a constructive line of thought and action which will have a lasting benefit for the reader.

To preserve the character of his spoken word the editing has been deliberately 'light'.

PR Oct 2017

This collection of lectures given by the late
Dr A. M. Halliday has been compiled for publication
*at the express wish of his late wife Elise (Lisl) Halliday**
to whom they were bequeathed in 2008.
This book is dedicated to her with deep gratitude.

*Lisl Halliday was one of the last living pupils of Hari Prasad Shastri. Dr Shastri established Shanti Sadan in London in 1933 as the first centre of Adhyatma Yoga in the West. Lisl became a pupil of Dr Shastri in 1941 and cared for him until his physical life drew to a close in 1956.

CONTENTS

INTRODUCTION

The themes of the following selection of lectures might be summarised as follows.

To live without an attempt at introspection is to risk spending one's life chasing ill-defined goals for ill-defined purposes. Are we following consciously decided goals or are we following them as chance presents them to us? Are we in charge of our mind or does our mind control us? The first step in rectifying this begins when we take time to properly assess our current situation.

It is the assertion of many, that far from being at the mercy of the mind we have the opportunity to train and refine it. In the following lectures this is explored according to the principles of Adhyatma Yoga. Whilst this Yoga has a venerable background and traditional texts to support it, the particular appeal of these lectures is that these principles have also been hinted at and expounded by much more recent thinkers from a broad spread of backgrounds such as the modern psychology of Erich Fromm, the spirituality of Isaac Penington and the pursuit of science by Isaac Newton.

When the training of Adhyatma Yoga is undertaken, the mind reveals its true basis – and far from being the originator of our consciousness it is really acting to give a poor and distorted reflection of the source of all consciousness or Self. It is by realising our identity with this Self that the riddle of life, full of apparent contradiction and paradox, is solved.

In the *Upanishads*, the ancient texts traditionally taken as commentaries on the Vedas, we are given four main principles of Adhyatma Yoga. Firstly, that the search for truth is a search not in the outer world but within your own self. Secondly, that the ultimate reality within your self cannot be known by any of the senses. Thirdly, that although it cannot be known by the senses it is knowable as a direct, unmediated experience. Fourthly, that the ultimate reality is the pure light of Consciousness.

The path of Adhyatma Yoga does not require unshakeable faith from the outset. Rather its propositions can be verified within one's own experience and are finally known as incontrovertibly true by direct experience. In this way it is 'scientific' in its approach to the psychological condition of man.

PR Oct 2017

1

The Greatest Acquisition*

IF WE LOOK at the history of mankind and ask ourselves what the human mind is like, what it is capable of, we shall find that it can produce on the one hand a Shakespeare, a Newton, a Christ or an Einstein, but also on the other hand it can, and has, produced a Hitler, a Nero, a Genghis Khan and a Machiavelli. What makes the difference, this different picture of what man can become? And is there a science by studying which we can make something better out of the human personality? These are the questions which we are considering, and it is our wish to present the teachings of Yoga, the classical spiritual Yoga, on this topic.

Now, spiritual teachers are not blind optimists nor are they disillusioned cynics. They tell us that the same basic human nature is common to all men, but that what makes the difference between one man and another man is the use which we make of that basic human nature.

The human mind, we can say, functions on a number of levels: the instinctive, the emotional, the rational, the aesthetic and the intuitive. By our habitual ways of thinking each and every one of us takes a stand on one or other of these levels in the mind, and we come as a consequence to rely on that level of the mind and to cultivate it.

One might say that each individual, according to the teaching of Yoga on this topic, is like a man owning

---

*A lecture given on 3rd December 1965.

and living in a multi-storeyed house. If he is not very adventurous, he may never go beyond the ground floor, in which case, although the house above is always there above his head, the upstairs rooms will be neglected and unused. When he needs to go there, or when he does go there eventually, it will be difficult because those rooms will be in disorder. There will be great gloom there, and everything will be covered by a pall of cobwebs and dust so that one can't really see clearly what the rooms contain or what possibilities there are to be made out of them.

But if that man, that householder, wants to enjoy his house to the full, and to have the benefit of all that it can offer him, then he'll be wise to learn from the outset to move freely and easily all round that house, moving not only between the rooms on one floor but from one floor to another as it is appropriate for him to do. We all know, of course, that even when he has done this, there will be some part of that house – and I think this is true of everybody – which is particularly his, the place that you'll expect to find him in if he has got nothing better to do, his own room, if you like.

It's the same, say the Yogis, with the mind, with the human personality. It too has many faculties which function, so to speak, on many different levels. In many people a lot of these faculties lie dormant and unused and perhaps that person who has them is hardly aware that they exist. They are like the upstairs rooms which are never visited. So the ideal, if we are to use the mind effectively, is that we can use all these mental faculties freely as and when they are needed.

Those who have studied the work of the Western psychologist Carl Gustav Jung will know that one of his doctrines is that human personalities can be divided into four great types according to faculty; these being thought, intellect, intuition, as well as feeling and sensation. And he says that individuals, in the Jungian view, differ according to which of these faculties they have developed. He says that in the majority of people only one faculty is well-developed. In the exceptional person two faculties may be developed but, he says, it's very rare to find a person who is so well integrated as a personality that they have three of these faculties well-developed and that they can use each of them equally well, still less likely someone who is able to use any of these faculties. Well, this is a parallel, a modern Jungian view, of something similar to what the Yogis are saying in this respect.

So the ideal is, if we are going to use the mind effectively, that we should be able to make use of any of the faculties that exist in it where they are needed, in the appropriate context. But even when we can, like the man who is able to move all round the house, there will, nonetheless, always be one particular part of our personality in which we are most at home, most frequently to be found, say the Yogis. And it is this level or part – a part in which we are established – on which we most rely, that constitutes in the yogic terminology our *bhava*. This is a very difficult word to translate, but it means the place where we are customarily established. I'm sure many of us know people who are customarily established in the faculty of argumentation. There are many people who are customarily established in the faculty of sensation, or even in one of the emotions, such as anger or irritability, and we characteristically associate such personalities with this particular mental state. These are not very good places to be established in, needless to say.

Now, we have to be somewhere in the house, the personality, so long as we are using the mind, say the Yogis.

And the great point which they make in the *Bhagavad Gita* and elsewhere is that, if we do not take our stand on the higher part of our being, the lower part of the mind will overpower it and we shall suffer the consequences. We'll suffer, if you like, a lower standard of living, not an economic standard, but a psychological and spiritual standard. Even without knowing the yogic teaching on this, we can perhaps see it in our own experience – there is an innate sense of this in everyone – and surely it's this which makes us all ashamed and annoyed when we find ourselves compromising our own internal integrity and happiness by lowering ourselves in our own eyes, by not acting up to that which we feel is our real nature, our real Self. And this is surely a recognition, however inarticulate or unconscious, of where we take our stand.

Now it's quite clear that different people take their stand in a quite different place. For instance, one doesn't find the same standard of honour in Falstaff in Shakespeare's Henry IV that one finds in Prince Hal or the King, and the fact that Falstaff doesn't live up to Prince Hal's standard of honour doesn't worry him in the slightest. But it would worry Prince Hal very much if he didn't live up to his own standards. So we can say that they have a different *bhava*, they have got a different place or part of the mind in which they are established. And this is the yogic doctrine on this particular point.

How are we to raise the standard of living, the psychological standard of living? This is the great question at the outset of Yoga. It can only be achieved by effort, say the Yogis, and in this field it has to be our own effort. It's no good, as when we complain about the low external standard of living, we have always someone else to blame; we can blame the Unions; we can blame mismanagement of the

Government; we can blame the state of the world, and so on, or the Depression. But in regard to our own standard of living, in regard to the internal part of the mind in which we are established, it's only our own effort which can raise or lower it, and as the Chinese sage, Confucius, says: 'Men's natures are alike; it is their habits which carry them far apart.' The great pupil of Confucius, Mencius, commenting on this verse of Confucius, says that by 'habit' Confucius here means that part of the mind, that part of the inner being, on which we habitually take our stand. He says, if you, from the outset, take your stand on the higher part of the mind, then the lower part of the mind will be powerless to rob you of that benefit. But if you habitually neglect this, then you lower your standard of living, so to speak, and you aren't able to make use of the faculties that the mind has in it. They remain inaccessible.

So we all start, according to Yoga, with the same raw material of human nature, the personality, and almost the only thing which we can be said to have free will over, to some extent, is the cultivation of our own personality. Though this raw material is given to us, we come into the world with the personality. What we make of it is the result of our own conscious choice, hundreds of thousands of choices over the whole of our life. Then why not be constructive and create something worthwhile out of it? This is the moral; something which is a gain to ourselves and a benefit to society as a whole. Why should we create the undesirable? Why should we create the man depicted in so many contemporary plays and films, rather than the man of the type, if you like, of Albert Schweitzer, or Danilo Dolci, of the artist, of the philosopher – something worthwhile in whatever field it is?

Some people will answer that the human personality is often fundamentally bad and that human nature is hopelessly flawed. But it is not so, according to the spiritual teachers. Shakespeare provides a picture of man which is not always flattering. But why do we go on reading Shakespeare? Why has Shakespeare lasted so many hundreds of years? He is not lacking in realism but he continually shows the nobility and the greatness and the humanity possible, even in the most insignificant of his characters. And we feel at once these characters are real people; they are alive and we can feel something of ourselves in them. They may be very different characters, but there is something we recognise in them which is like our own experience.

The modern playwrights, since this is a time of disillusionment, no doubt reflect the dominant view nowadays. In the main they show man only as a worm and worse than a worm, but what we have to remember is that even a worm, given the choice, would prefer not to be a worm, which shows that in each and every worm there is a feeling of excellence and a love of greatness and this in itself shows that even a worm wishes to transcend its worminess! Well, this is perhaps taking the analogy too far. But we can see how much more true this is of man. The best has an innate attraction for each and everyone, even when they become disillusioned. So the question is, why don't we follow it?

We start life with certain predispositions and certain gifts. It is not said that every individual is exactly the same. Certainly not. From the psychological point of view there are many differences between individual and individual. But like the man with the talents in the parable in the New Testament, we each have potentialities and those potentialities are for greatness as well as for littleness, or for goodness as well as for badness. And the question is how to make the most of them. How to create something worthwhile out of these talents that we have. Yoga aims, in its own words, to teach each man to live more skilfully, to express the best of which he is capable and to reveal the seed of perfection which is in him, as in each and every other man.

Well, you may say, this is very interesting but this teaching is only for a few and most people ignore it. It may be so, but there is a great danger if we ignore the spiritual teaching, if we ignore, not only the teaching as it comes to us in Yoga, but also as it comes to us in our own Western tradition. Because the mind, if it is not a friend, can become a great enemy. We live, so to speak, on the top of a metaphorical volcano – the destructive propensities of our own unspiritualised mind – and there is no knowing, if we neglect it, when it may erupt. If you like, in the basement of the house there is a potentially anarchic and revolutionary rebel who will come and take over, if the owner is lazy and adopts a policy of laissez-faire. So that the mind is neglected, these truths about the mind are neglected at our peril, and it's worth taking trouble now to listen to what the Yogis say, because what they tell us is that we have it in our power to transform the mind into a creative force, channelled into beneficent directions.

One of the similes given in the yogic classics of the mind is that it is like a frozen dragon. If we allow it to be unfrozen, without being wise and transforming it first into a friend, without being able to control it first, then it will be a great destructive force. You can't afford to unfreeze the dragon of the mind, so to speak, until you can control it.

It's worth remembering that Napoleon in his youth was a very ambitious man but he was ambitious to do a great deal of good, and one of the essays he wrote, which we still have, was an essay against ambition. He had genuine philanthropic desires in his early days, but these all became lost once results began to come and he got more and more power in his hands. In the end he became interested only in one thing, conquest, conquest, conquest and getting more men from France. Even when a large proportion of the population had been killed in his previous wars, his one idea was to go on conquering other countries. So this is an example of the mind running away when we don't spiritualise and control it.

How then are we to live fully and wisely? Doing justice to the best that our personality is capable of expressing? The reply of Yoga is, only by conscious living, only by effort, by training ourselves in the right use of the mind.

So many people nowadays are enthusiastic about physical training. If you go into Regent's Park at almost any time, you find people running round in track suits, even in the coldest weather, even sometimes in the rain! There is tremendous interest in physical training. It may be for athletic achievement or it may be for aesthetic considerations. After all, think how rigidly people are willing to diet, whether to be fit or not to be fat. How eagerly and painstakingly people will buy clothes to adorn the body. If one went into it, I think there must now be a very considerable annual expenditure on cosmetics, on hairdressers and on various forms of beauty treatment. Well, it's interesting to consider, because it shows beyond question that people are really interested in looking after the body, and that they are really willing to sacrifice both money and time, and a great deal of both, to the cultivation of the body and in some cases also to its training. But then, what about the mind?

Isn't it ridiculous that we don't worry about the diet of the mind and its adornment, that we hardly ever give a thought to the training of this, in some ways, much more important faculty that we possess, this much more important instrument of ours? On the contrary, when one looks at the majority of films and newspapers that we feed the mind on, one can say that the diet is little better, metaphorically speaking, than pigs' swill, or at any rate the cheapest and worst of sweets. These may seem strong words, but just consider the content of a good deal of the press, or look on a railway bookstall at a good deal of the matter which is on sale. No wonder then, if we neglect it so much, that the mind goes flabby so often and perhaps suffers prematurely from middle-age spread. We aren't surprised when this happens to the body; why should we be surprised when it happens to the mind if we feed that too on the wrong food?

Well, Yoga calls itself the science of skilful living and it teaches us that we cannot afford to neglect the mind in this way, that we have to know how to control the mind and to convert it into a really useful instrument. And the yogic methods provide the necessary techniques for the mental and spiritual training of the personality.

But what I have said so far may lead you to suppose that the aim of Yoga is simply to get a more integrated personality, simply to have better control of the mind. And this is not at all the case. The real aim of Yoga is to enable the individual to answer the central problem of life. You'll ask, what is that central problem? Over the gate of the Oracle at Delphi was written: 'Know Thyself'. It was considered the paramount question, the only wisdom really worth having by the ancient Greeks. Well, you'll say, that was a very long time ago. We are now over two millennia away from the time of Socrates and Plato. Have we not discarded this idea? And I would simply quote in answer from the words of one of the greatest scientists of his century, Erwin Schrödinger, who is the father of quantum mechanics. This is what he says: 'The scope, aim and value of natural science is the same as that of any other branch of human knowledge, nay none of them alone, only the union of all of them has any scope or value at all, and that is simply enough described. It is to obey the command of the Delphic oracle, to get to know yourself.' Well, this is the view of one of the greatest contemporary scientists.

Yoga, then, aims to answer this question, to give man Self-knowledge, an answer to the question 'what am I?' And it points out that when this enquiry is pursued and the Self is known, it is discovered to be a spiritual entity, not the local self but the divine ray, so to speak, of the eternal consciousness in which the whole world lives, moves and has its being. This is so, in a very real and different sense, in Schrödinger's equation, where he says that the aim of science (which after all wants to know the reality behind the world, wants to know what is the fundamental reality behind the world) and the Delphic oracle's command 'Know Thyself', are one and the same. In the case of the yogic enquiry, the reality in man is the same as the spiritual reality behind the world.

The teachings of Yoga about the nature of this spiritual principle can be summed up in four cardinal doctrines or points. Though the teaching of Yoga is very ancient (it is first promulgated in the *Upanishads*, which are some of the earliest books that have come down to us) it is still practised and still has great Yogis who have realised this knowledge in the present day. The tradition of the techniques has been handed down continuously from teacher to pupil during that time. I will take, to illustrate the four points, some texts from a very early work on Yoga, the *Mundaka Upanishad*. They show that the doctrine has not changed. The first point is that this reality is to be sought within the personality of man as the innermost Self. In the *Upanishad* there is the verse:[1]

> 'The multitude of souls have come forth from this immortal reality like so many sparks issuing forth from a flaming fire and they find their way back into it. He who knows this highest reality, the immortal, as seated in the innermost heart of man, for such a man the knot of spiritual ignorance is untied even here in this life.'

This is the first point then, that this reality is not to be sought outside, is not to be sought in some transcendental heaven, but is within the innermost heart of man. As Shri Krishna says in the *Bhagavad Gita*: 'O Arjuna, know that I, the Lord, am seated in the hearts of all beings, in the sinner as much as in the saint.'[2] And you will remember in our own Western tradition the saying of St Paul: 'Know ye not that ye are temples of God for the spirit of God dwelleth in you?'

The second point is that this reality cannot be known by the senses. It is altogether beyond their range. Nor can it be adequately described by words. Again a verse from the *Upanishad* illustrates this: 'He is not grasped by the eye, nor by speech, nor by the other senses, nor by austerity, nor good works.' This reality can't be known as we know an object. We can't expect to see it under the microscope or through the telescope of the astronomer. It is a spiritual reality within the mind. When the Buddha was asked by one of his disciples to describe the nature of the spiritual truth he

---

[1] *Mundaka Upanishad* II.i.1and II.i.10.

[2] *Bhagavad Gita* X, 20; XIII, 17; XV, 15 and XVIII, 61

remained silent. The disciple repeated his question and still the Buddha remained silent. A third time the disciple asked him to explain, then the Buddha turned to him and said: 'I am telling you the answer but you do not hear.' This is an illustration of the inability of this reality to be expressed in objective terms, in terms of speech and description through the senses. In one of the other *Upanishads* occurs the verse:[3] 'It is from whence speech and the mind turn baffled back again.'

The third point is that although this is so, it is not, therefore, unknowable. It can be realised through the purified mind, not as an idea or an object, but as that reality in which the mind lives and moves and has its being. Again I quote a verse:[4] 'When one's mind is purified by the clearness of knowledge, then alone he sees the indivisible reality through meditation.' Here in this verse the means to this knowledge are indicated. It is through the purification and concentration of the mind leading to clear vision, to 'the clearness of knowledge', as the verse calls it, when one's mind is purified by the clearness of knowledge, then alone he sees the indivisible reality through meditation.

The fourth point is that this reality in man, this real Self of man, is the pure light of Consciousness within and behind the mind. Again another verse from the *Mundaka Upanishad*:[5] 'The stainless indivisible reality, the pure, the light of all lights, is within the innermost layer of the personality.' Here the *Upanishad* speaks of the layers of the personality. This corresponds to the floors of the multi-storeyed house of the personality in our previous analogy – within the innermost layer of the personality.

---

[3] *Taittirya Upanishad* II.ix.1.

[4] *Mundaka Upanishad* III.i.8.

[5] *Mundaka Upanishad* II.ii.19.

That is what the Self-realised Yogis know: 'The sun shines not there, nor the moon and stars, nor do these lightnings shine, what to say of fire; all shine in His light; all this is illumined by His radiance.'[6] The meaning is that consciousness is prior to all sensation. First of all one feels 'I am', and so the great dictum of Descartes: 'I think therefore I am'. Without 'I am' there is no possibility either of thinking or of perceiving or of knowing or of experiencing. So, first of all, there is the light of self-awareness. All shines in His light, the light of His self-awareness.

Well, these are the four points which summarise the central doctrine of Yoga in this respect. At the beginning of the *Mundaka Upanishad* which I have been quoting, that great householder, Sanaka, approaches the teacher Angiras and he says: 'Sir, what is that through which if it is known everything else becomes known? What is that truth, what is the thing really worth knowing?' he asks the teacher.

After all, by knowing Newton's laws all mechanics really becomes comprehensible; almost all mechanics is deducible from the laws of Newton. In chemistry, when one knows the periodic table of Mendeleyev, then one can predict many of the properties of the different elements and the way they will interact with each other.

What is that by knowing which everything else becomes known? That is the question. Is there anything so fundamental that it enlightens all things and makes them explicable is the question? And the reply is: Yes, there is – it is a knowledge of the spiritual truth, the truth which when known makes man free. Angiras reveals to Sanaka that there are actually two kinds of knowledge, direct and indirect. We can call them theoretical knowledge and experience. A man may be very well informed – he may indeed have

---

[6] *Mundaka Upanishad* II.ii.20.

an encyclopaedic knowledge of theoretical facts but this is a very different thing from having experience. It doesn't mean at all that he is a man of wide experience.

Let us take as an example a man who has never tasted a peach. If he goes to a botanist and asks what a peach is like, the botanist will tell him a great deal about it. He can tell him that it is the fruit of a tree, that it is a tree of the Rosaceae family, that it is a species of prunus and that its Latin name is *Prunus persica*. We can well ask whether the man will be any better off. He is perhaps better off in asking the next person about it because he has the wherewithal to do a little bit of one-upmanship on the next person he asks, but as regards actually knowing anything about the peach, he is really not much better off than he was to begin with. So let's suppose he gives up the botanist and goes to a nutrition expert, a nutrition scientist. Well, in response to his question, what is a peach, no scientist will ever say he doesn't know, particularly if he is employed by the Ministry of Food! He will no doubt be told that the peach is eighty per cent water, five per cent carbohydrate and a little bit of protein, practically no fat, some mineral traces and a great deal of cellulose.

Well again, what will the man know about the peach? He'll be slightly better off if he can meet someone who has actually tasted a peach because he at least will be able to tell him, if only in words, what the peach tastes like. He can tell him for instance that it's a bit like a plum, only softer, but it's not as acid as a plum, that it is sometimes not entirely unlike a pear, but it is not, on the other hand, quite the same flavour as a pear and that a very good Cox's Orange Pippin has something of the same flavour in it! Well, the problem here is that he can only describe it to the man in terms of what he has already experienced. It's much nearer to the true description of the peach but it is still what the teacher calls 'indirect knowledge', and theoretical knowledge or 'indirect knowledge' is very inadequate. How can he explain something to someone who has not known anything like it themselves? He can only hint at it in terms which the other man already understands, and these may be quite inadequate – in other words, it can only be conveyed by analogy.

We are up against the same difficulty, say the Yogis, in regard to spiritual experience spoken of by the masters. The saints and mystics tell us that they have verified this experience for themselves and they testify to the truth of the existence of the spiritual reality which is described. We can gain confidence because we find such a surprising unanimity amongst the mystics of all ages and climes and quite different traditions, many of whom had no means of knowing about the writings of the others, often in different parts of the world with which there was no communication. But still all this is only indirect knowledge. As St Paul says, we know now only in part. We see only, so to speak, through a glass darkly some glimpses of the spiritual reality in these testimonies and also in those rare and valued moments of heightened awareness which come to most men on occasions. What we need to know is the truth face-to-face, to know even as we are known.

The Yogis can only explain their experience to us indirectly in terms that we can understand, in terms of our everyday experience and in terms of our familiar mental conceptions and images. But they stress, one and all, that the important thing is that each and every one has within them the capacity to verify that experience for themselves and this is the purpose of the teachings of Yoga which they give. 'Not by long study of the scriptures, not by agile feats of intellect, not by obedient listening to the wise cometh the spirit,'[7] says the *Upanishad*, 'To him alone the spirit shall be given who thirsteth for it, who wooeth it untiringly, to such a seeking soul in very sooth the spirit cometh.'

It is only by making experiments, by attaining to a personal verification of the facts that this riddle, this central problem of life, will ultimately be solved. When the great Sufi mystic Al-Ghazali was a great secular scholar early in his career, before he had turned to the spiritual path, he was travelling with a caravan of donkeys all of which were loaded with books. The caravan was set upon by a band of robbers and the robbers were curious at such an extraordinary load and the man who had it. They asked him what he was and he said he was a scholar. And they said, 'What do you want all these books for?' He said, 'These are the things that I study – my knowledge is in these books.' And they said, 'It's not very good knowledge if you don't know it without the books.' This had a great effect on Al-Ghazali and it was one of the factors which made him become a great spiritual figure. He was determined to get the spiritual knowledge which is not something contained in books, not something which one can be separated from once one has it, because it is a matter of direct experience. It is the same point.

The man searching for the peach must sooner or later find a fruit gardener, a man who knows or has peaches himself, who is familiar with the peach and who knows each variety, which is the most sweet and when it should be eaten. The seeker may be offered dried peaches, and he may imagine when he has had them, this is the real peach. But it is not the real thing at all. If he finds a genuine gardener he'll laugh at him when he describes the dried peach. The dried peaches, say the Yogis, are all the things

---

[7] *Katha Upanishad* I.ii.23 / *Mundaka Upanishad* III.ii.3.

that are offered to the Yogi in the course of his training, the psychic perfections, the mental powers, and so on, which you will see described in many books. From the point of view of the spiritual quest, these are merely dried peaches. They are merely things masquerading as the real goal of Yoga and they are not worth having. They are ultimately a disappointment and they are merely diversions from the real search for the peach. Once he has tasted the peach, once he has been told by the gardener where he can find the peach, and he has been sent there, and he has picked the peach for himself and eaten it from the tree, he doesn't need any descriptions because he has a direct knowledge of it. In fact, he knows that no descriptions can adequately describe that characteristic, succulent and delicious aroma of the peach to one who has not known it.

So it is, the Yogis tell us, with the yogic knowledge: personal experience is the essential thing. However much learning you may have about Yoga or about the spiritual path, it will not do you a great deal of good unless you have experienced the yogic realisation for yourself. It is a path of light, as the *Upanishad* says, to be travelled, not simply to be studied on a map. And even a little travel will teach you more and widen your horizon and give you more understanding and a deeper peace and light in the mind, than any amount of theoretical knowledge of the yogic literature from the outside, so to speak. As the Chinese Taoists say: the way that is subject to discussion is not the true way.

This path of light described in the *Mundaka Upanishad* leads then to the knowledge of the real Self of man. Two verses from the *Upanishad* describe this goal:[8]

[8] *Mundaka Upanishad* III.i.6–7.

'Truth alone wins, not falsehood. By truth the path of light is widened, that by which the Yogis travel on, having nothing to wish for, to where there is that, the highest treasure attained by truth; that shines as vast, heavenly, of unthinkable form and subtler than the subtlest, much further than the distant, near also here and seen established within the heart by the wise.'

2

Search and Self-Discovery*

IN 1951, a scientist who is perhaps among the greatest figures in twentieth century physics, Erwin Schrödinger, wrote these words:[9]

> 'I am born into an environment – I know not whence I came, nor whither I go, nor who I am. This is my situation as yours, every single one of you. The fact that everyone always was in this same situation...tells me nothing. Our burning question as to the whence and whither – all we can ourselves observe about it is the present environment. That is why we are eager to find out about it as much as we can. That is science, learning, knowledge, that is the true source of every spiritual endeavour of man.'

For Schrödinger this is the central problem facing man, the problem of self-knowledge, and it can and must be tackled here and now just where we stand. Science, with its aim of discovering more about the nature of the world around us, is simply one aspect of this search for self-knowledge. And its ultimate value is to be judged, not as a source of

---

*A lecture given on 15th October 1966.

[9]*Science and Humanism*, lectures given by Schrödinger in Dublin in 1950, Cambridge University Press, 1951.

power or economic prosperity, but by its contribution to an understanding of ourselves. As Schrödinger says:[10]

> 'The scope, aim and value of science is the same as that of any other branch of human knowledge. Nay, none of them alone, only the union of all of them, has any scope or value at all, and that is simply enough described: it is to obey the command of the Delphic oracle, get to know yourself.'

You will remember that the command 'Know Thyself' was inscribed over the gate of the Oracle at Delphi, so that all who entered should read and remember it.

The search for knowledge, then, according to Schrödinger, whether in science or any other department of human endeavour, is ultimately the search for Self-knowledge. But Schrödinger is making another valuable point when he adds:[11]

> 'It seems plain and self-evident, yet it needs to be said: the isolated knowledge obtained by a group of specialists in a narrow field has in itself no value whatsoever, but only in its synthesis with all the rest of knowledge and only inasmuch as it really contributes in this synthesis something towards answering the demand: "Who are we?"'

Now Yoga may well be regarded (to use Schrödinger's phrase) as 'the isolated knowledge obtained by a group of specialists in a narrow field', but it can claim to make a

---

[10]*Science and Humanism*, lectures given by Schrödinger in Dublin in 1950, Cambridge University Press, 1951, p. 4.

[11]*Science and Humanism*, lectures given by Schrödinger in Dublin in 1950, Cambridge University Press, 1951, p. 4.

unique contribution to the quest for Self-knowledge, since this is the deliberate and avowed aim of its discipline and practice. Therefore, if the ultimate value of any discipline is to be judged by how much it helps us towards Self-knowledge, and if the claim of Yoga is just, it has a very special value for man in his search, even today in modern Western civilisation.

Schrödinger is, indeed, only echoing the Yogis when he says that the most fundamental and pressing question facing each and every individual is: 'What am I?' However, questions are only asked so that they can be answered and, as Aldous Huxley pointed out,[12] we are not all equally good at answering them.

> 'Because we are free [he says] it is possible for us to answer life's questions either well or badly. If we answer them badly, we shall bring down upon ourselves self-stultification. Most often this self-stultification will take subtle and not immediately detectable forms, as when our failure to answer properly makes it impossible for us to realise the higher potentialities of our being. Sometimes, on the contrary, the self-stultification is manifest on the physical level and may involve not only individuals as individuals, but entire societies, which go down in catastrophe or sink more slowly into decay. The giving of correct answers is rewarded primarily by spiritual growth and progressive realisation of latent potentialities, and secondarily (when circumstances make it possible) by adding of all the rest to the realised Kingdom of God.'

---

[12]Aldous Huxley, *The Perennial Philosophy*, Harper & Brothers, 1945 (original work published pre-1945, year unknown).

I have quoted at length from those two Western thinkers to show that they too are in agreement with the teachers of Yoga, that the most important goal of life is Self-knowledge and that the way we answer the question 'What am I?' has vital consequences for our own life and happiness, for our own inner freedom or bondage. And yet Yoga has something quite different to contribute to this problem than the scientist has or, indeed, any other of the disciplines through which man seeks knowledge or self-expression. For, as Schrödinger says, all that the scientist can do in his attempt to answer the burning questions of what he is, whence he came and whither he is going, is to observe and investigate 'the present environment'. 'All we can observe about it,' he says, 'is the present environment.'

Note this point of Schrödinger's well for it is of fundamental importance. Even if, by means of physiology and psychology, we extend the scientific investigation to the inner environment, to the *milieu intérieur*, to unravel the mechanisms of the brain and the functions of the mind, from the point of view of Yoga we are still limited to the environment, to the realm of the experienced, and have not turned our attention within to the experiencing entity, the Self. Science investigates the world around us and, albeit more haltingly, the mental world which surrounds us internally, but it does not manage to capture the Self on the stage of its examining microscope because the Self is the one looking into the microscope.

What is this Self, the experiencer and witness of the moods and states of the mind, no less than of the perceptions brought to it by the five senses? It is a problem upon which there have been many conflicting views in the history of philosophy. Some, like the Madhyamika School of Buddhists and David Hume in the Western tradition, have believed that there was no such thing as the Self, that it was only an appearance set up by the succession of ever-changing states of the mind, like the appearance of reality set up by the succession of pictures projected onto a screen in a cinema. Some have believed on the contrary that the Self was just what it appears to be – a person acting and suffering and enjoying, owning property and seeking the well-being of the body and mind which it regards as its own. There are thus many theories about the Self and, if there is no means of deciding between them, everyone is perhaps equally entitled to his own opinion. Although, as Huxley points out, the way we answer this question is not only of theoretical interest, it has practical consequences too.

But there is, quite apart from differences of opinion, the question as to which of the views is true. This is independent of the opinion or who holds it. Now whatever people may choose to believe about spiritual teaching nowadays, its aim and object is a knowledge of truth, not an acceptance of some helpful or unhelpful beliefs. It is really concerned with freeing man from the fantasy world created by his own ignorance, and from the crude and superstitious distortions of truth produced by his own lower mind.

The real bondage of man, according to the great spiritual teachers, is the bondage to his instinctive, sense-loving, individualistic tendencies, and the real freedom is freedom from this bondage to the lower mind. It only comes with wisdom and enlightenment, and certainly does not come simply from intellectual knowledge. When Christ said: 'Know ye the Truth and the Truth shall make you free', his statement was at once treated with incredulity by his hearers, who said to him: 'But we have never been bond-slaves to any man. Why do you talk about freeing us?' His reply was that every man who sinned was a bond-slave to sin. In other words, that everyone who was at the mercy of their own lower mind and unbridled instincts was anything but free, and that only a knowledge of the spiritual Truth, conferring wisdom and enlightenment, could free them.

Nowadays, when religious teaching is unfashionable and supposedly discredited, many people would rather seek help from the psychoanalyst than the saint. But they may find they are only getting the same message in more contemporary jargon. Listen to the American psychoanalyst Erich Fromm, for instance, as he gives a picture of the contemporary human situation.

> 'In the modern world, [he says] our society is run by a managerial bureaucracy, by professional politicians; people are motivated by mass suggestion, their aim is producing more and consuming more, as purposes in themselves. All activities are subordinated to economic goals, means have become ends; man is an automaton – well fed, well clad, but without any ultimate concern for that which is his human quality and function. If man is to be able to love, he must be put in his supreme place. The economic machine must serve him, rather than he serve it.[13] ...Automatons cannot love, they can only exchange their "personality packages" and hope for a fair bargain.'[14]

Fromm's theme is that a society based on love is the only sane and satisfactory answer to the problem of human existence – something which Shri Krishna, Buddha and Christ all said thousands of years ago. For Fromm the art of loving requires maturity, spiritual as well as moral and physical, and modern man is still infantile in his attitude.

---

[13]Erich Fromm, *The Art of Loving*, Harper & Brothers, 1956, p. 94.
[14]Erich Fromm, *The Art of Loving*, Harper & Brothers, 1956, p. 64.

> 'Modern man is actually close to the picture Huxley describes in his Brave New World: well fed, well clad, satisfied sexually, yet without self, without any except the most superficial contact with his fellow men, guided by slogans such as "Never put off till tomorrow the fun you can have today". Man's happiness today consists in "having fun". Having fun consists in the satisfaction of consuming and "taking in" commodities, sights, food, drinks, cigarettes, people, lectures, books, movies – all are consumed, swallowed. The world is one great object for our appetite, we are the eternally expectant ones, the hopeful ones – and the eternally disappointed ones. Our character is geared to exchange and to receive, to barter and to consume; everything, spiritual as well as material objects, becomes an object of exchange and consumption.'[15]

Long ago, that great classic of Yoga, the *Bhagavad Gita*, was saying: 'The deluded ones think: today I have gained this wealth and position; that I shall obtain in the future; this is mine now and that will be mine. Unbalanced in mind on account of numerous imaginary and selfish projects, ambitions and desires, (they are) imprisoned in the net of infatuation (and personal attachments).'[16]

This is indeed a real kind of bondage – but a bondage which has its seat not so much in the outer circumstances as in our own state of mind. It is, above all, the result of answering the question 'Who am I?' in a particular way. If we believe that the individual is no more than a cog in the machine, one insignificant ant in the anthill of human

---

[15]Erich Fromm, *The Art of Loving*, Harper & Brothers, 1956, p. 64.
[16]*Bhagavad Gita* XVI, 13 and XVI, 16.

society, then certain consequences follow. If we are no more than the body then the good of the body becomes our greatest good, and its well-being and gratification is the only legitimate object of life. The pursuit of sense-pleasure and comfort, blatant individualism and narrow self-interest, will become the driving force in life for those who hold such a view. But their outlook will be infantile from the spiritual point of view, because it denies all that makes man man. It is the teaching of Yoga that man must become not only physically adult, but also spiritually adult as well. He will not do so, however, so long as his growth is stunted by a false and limited view of his own being and its potentialities.

Development and expansion must go on if he is to obey the law of growth which is inborn in his being, but eventually he has to turn within to the sphere of his inner being. He has first to develop and awaken his aesthetic and moral sensibilities, and this is an important field for expansion but there is something beyond even this, the spiritual element in his being.

Einstein, though no orthodox believer, hints at this reality, the source of all true mysticism, in his own personal credo. He hints at it as a man who senses the existence of such a reality, but has no means of contacting it. He lacks any experimental technique of investigation. He already acknowledges himself as a lover of the moral and aesthetic ideals, but he can only praise the spiritual ideal as an outsider, so to speak. Here is something of what he says:[17]

> '...everyone holds certain ideals by which he guides his aspiration and his judgment. The ideals which have always shone before me and filled me with the joy of

[17]Albert Einstein, *Living Philosophies*, Simon and Schuster, 1931, p. 27.

> living are goodness, beauty and truth. To make a goal of comfort or happiness has never appealed to me; a system of ethics built on this basis would be sufficient only for a herd of cattle. Ever since childhood I have scorned the commonplace limits so often set upon human ambition. Possession, outward success, publicity, luxury – to me these have always been contemptible. I believe that a simple and unassuming manner of life is best for everyone, best both for the body and the mind.'

This much outlines Einstein's ideas on the social, ethical and aesthetic ideals of life, but he has something more to say, when he reaches out to join the ranks of the great mystics and Yogis.

> 'The most beautiful thing we can experience is the mysterious. It is the source of all true art and science... and has also given rise to religion. To know that what is impenetrable to us really exists, manifesting itself as the highest wisdom and the most radiant beauty which our dull faculties can comprehend only in their most primitive forms – this knowledge, this feeling, is at the centre of true religiousness. In this sense, and in this sense only, I belong in the ranks of devoutly religious men.'[18]

Einstein is here expressing the intuition of a higher reality behind and within all, transcending the realm accessible to the senses or reason: 'To know that what is impenetrable to us really exists.'

There are two points here, both equally vital: that it exists and that it is impenetrable for the scientist or the intellectual. If it is impenetrable to us how do we know that

---

[18]Albert Einstein, *Living Philosophies*, Simon and Schuster, 1931.

it really exists? We do not know unless we have verified it in our own experience. But let us make no mistake. The teaching of Yoga and of all mystical traditions is that this Reality does exist. The Yogis therefore have no truck with the pragmatic view of religious Truth, that 'Truth is simply anything that it pays to believe', as Russell puts it; that religious teaching is to be accepted, not because it corresponds to any fact in the real world, but because the results of believing it are good for human individuals and human society.

Yoga teaches that the reality is present in every individual as the true Self, his real 'I'. Its discovery is the final answer to the question 'What am I?', the ultimate self-discovery, however other inadequate but plausible views of the nature of the Self obscure it for us.

The real Self is not 'impenetrable' to us, even though it was Einstein who said it was, for it can be realised through Yoga.

The *Bhagavad Gita*, Chapter VI (v 24-28), gives us this message:

> 'Abandoning without reserve all fancy-born desires, well restraining all the senses from all quarters by the mind; little by little let him withdraw, by reason *(buddhi)* held in firmness; keeping the mind established in the Self, let him not think of anything.
>
> 'By whatever cause the wavering and unsteady mind wanders away, from that let him restrain it and bring it back direct under the control of the Self.
>
> 'Supreme Bliss verily comes to this Yogin, whose mind is quite tranquil, whose passion is quieted, who has become Brahman, who is blemishless.

'Thus always keeping the self steadfast, the Yogin, freed from sins, attains with ease to the infinite bliss of contact with the (Supreme) Brahman.'

3

The Inner Light*

IF WE SEE someone whom we recognise to be really talented, wasting his talents, we feel what a shame it is. Many of us perhaps have had the experience of seeing someone young who is obviously gifted in some way – it may be artistically or with his hands, or the flair for some subject, for languages or science, for instance – but someone who, in spite of those talents, is still hardly aware of the gifts which he possesses. For want of encouragement and for want of someone making a small effort to create the right opportunities, those potentialities may come to nothing, and the man may never realise what he has missed or what a contribution he might have made. There is a stage in which it only needs a very little effort but it needs that effort to change the direction of a life. If the effort is made at the right time then the thing grows naturally.

Well, one meets cases such as these and one meets, which is sadder, cases later of people who have missed such opportunities. But the man who meets them at the right time and who recognises these talents will want to try and help the gifted person by telling him of the potentialities which he is not as yet realising. When Kathleen Ferrier was in her twenties she was, as you may know, still a telephone operator in Lancashire. She thought of herself as musical, but she thought of herself as a pianist, not as a singer, and

*A lecture given on 5th May 1967.

she had no idea that she had a voice which was exceptional, if not unique. It was only through the encouragement which she received from her friends in the first place, and later from her teachers, that those gifts as a singer were eventually realised in their full stature.

Here is another example: Sir Thomas Beecham was once having dinner at a restaurant in which a band was playing. He heard the violinist who was leading the band, and he recognised that here was a man with exceptional gifts as a violinist even though he was only playing in an ordinary restaurant orchestra. He sent a note to the man and he asked him to come and play for him. This is the way in which the career of Albert Sandler, who became one of the great violinists of the 1920s and 1930s, started. Simply at the right time someone recognised the potentialities and made the right gesture.

It is the same, in a certain sense, with each and every man. Each individual has some potential within him, but how much of this potential is realised or unrealised depends on him and on the circumstances. Of course, everybody knows that nature does not distribute the same empirical gifts to each person. Some people may have a talent for music, some people for painting, some for writing, some for philanthropy, some perhaps a talent for friendship, for real friendship. Some may appear to have very few empirical assets. But the spiritual teachers come to tell us that each and every individual has a potential greatness of which he is unaware, not simply in the empirical realm but also in the spiritual realm, and that it is in his own power to realise this potential fully. There is a great difference between the spiritual potential of an individual and his empirical potential. We can say that man's physical and intellectual talents vary from individual to individual, and whether they are latent or developed, they are not the same because the mind of each individual and his body, let alone his circumstances, are different. Everyone's mind is different and our physical bodies are also different.

From the spiritual point of view, however, each and every one has the same potential to realise his own spiritual perfection, because each and every one has innately, as his essence, one and the same spiritual nature. 'O Arjuna', says the Lord in the *Bhagavad Gita*, the great scripture of Yoga, 'I abide deep in the heart of each and every man.'[19] The spiritual training, then, of which Yoga is one path, aims at enabling each individual to realise his spiritual potential, to become consciously aware of his spiritual nature and, in doing so, to express what is best and highest in him. This spiritual potentiality is what is known by the mystics as 'the inner light'. In the *Upanishad* it says: 'He shining, all else shines.' The meaning is that the real spiritual essence of man is manifest as the light of consciousness in the innermost being of man. And according to the Yogis, the greatest good that any man can do is to awaken his latent spiritual faculties and uncover this inner light within himself.

People will say, if this is present in every man, why is it not apparent? The answer given by the Yogis is that it is not apparent because it is obscured by the darkness and opacity of the ignorant mind. Again I quote from the *Gita*: 'As smoke covers the light of a fire, so is the light of wisdom obscured by the darkness of unwisdom.'[20] The mind is like a flame by whose light man sees either dimly or clearly. What makes this flame smoky? Why is it a smoky flame whose light is darkened and covered? It is, to use the same simile, simply the bad quality of the fuel which is being fed into it.

---

[19] *Bhagavad Gita* X, 20; XIII, 17; XV, 15 and XVIII, 61.

[20] *Bhagavad Gita* III, 38-39.

One of the great criticisms, from the yogic point of view, of the modern fashions of thought is that in modern life people are encouraged in so many different ways to be sensation seekers, to be as they say ‘out for kicks’. Everyone seeks some kind of liberation from the confines of their everyday life and their dull everyday round. Each and every man tries to find such a release, but the current fashionable way of finding such release is by assaulting the senses. We can say that the popular view now is that one can only do this by assaulting the senses and the mind with drugs, by assaulting them in the cinema with scenes of violence or sadism or perversion or with any other things which are really assaults on the mind, which give a great shock to the emotional constitution of man. This is thought by many people to be the best way of seeking an escape from the dullness of everyday life.

From the spiritual point of view it is a very perverted taste. It is, we can say, rather like trying to get drunk by drinking methylated spirits or absinthe. Not only is it a bad drink in itself, not only is it distasteful, but also the result of it is, that eventually it destroys the faculties of perception. When I was in Glasgow, I saw many cases of these people who were so poor and desperate and miserable that they drank methylated spirits. In some cases they would place a glass of milk under the gas jets and bubble gas through it and drink the milk. Well, by analogy, one can say that this is the same kind of escape as we try to achieve psychologically by assaulting the mind or by assaulting the senses. In the end it coarsens the mind and renders it less and less responsive, until gradually it loses even the ability to respond to this shock effect. Even the scenes of violence, even the scenes which shock, no longer have any effect, so even for what it tries to achieve, it is self-stultifying. It is, from the spiritual point of view, a great perversion and a great mistake because this is not the way in which man can achieve a feeling of expansion or a feeling of liberation.

The spiritual teachers tell us that what we need to do is not to coarsen the mind, but to refine the mind and make it more sensitive. Only with a sensitive film can you accurately record the multivariegated hues and tones of the natural scene. A dull mind, like a poor film, sees things only in black and white. One can say it is not sensitive to the gradations of colour. Similarly, the mind which is ignorant, which is unrefined, which is coarsened, sees things only in terms of prejudice, as black or white. And this is what the Yogis mean when they speak of the mind being like a smoky flame in which wisdom is covered by unwisdom.

So the first point made by Yoga is that the truth is to be appreciated in its fullness. If we are really going to be lovers of truth as we should be, then it requires a highly sensitive mind, responsive to the subtlest differences. We can only achieve that mind if we feed into the mind the right fuel. The mind, says Patanjali, the great sage of Yoga, in order to qualify for the spiritual truth has to be *'rethambara'*, has to be adept at meditation on subtle things. It has to become hypersensitive, more sensitive, like a hypersensitive film, refined and able to grasp subtle things. All of us appreciate great dramatists like Shakespeare or Chekhov because of this sensitivity, because they respond, without prejudice and without judging, to every kind of human being which they portray.

In *Three Sisters*, Chekhov shows the apparent meaninglessness and triviality of ordinary life and the waste of human beings which it involves. At the end of the play the three sisters of the title are left together, having achieved nothing of what they had hoped, their money squandered by their weak brother who has married a social climber and taken to gambling, and Chekhov points out the theme for his audience, the theme 'what is the purpose of life?' One of the sisters says in almost the last speech: 'One day people will know what this is all for; what all this suffering is for, and nothing will be hidden.' Chekhov's view is not cynical, a disillusionment; on the contrary, he is at pains to show that the sisters feel that things can and will be different; that there should be joy even if they themselves have not achieved it. As the curtain falls they hear a band playing offstage, and the eldest sister Olga is saying: 'Let us live. The music is so happy, so full of joy. Surely before long we will know why we live and why we suffer. If only we knew, if only we knew.' From the spiritual point of view, life only begins when we ask ourselves this question. Then, if we think about it, we shall arrive at the conclusion that life is not purposeless but that it only seems purposeless to us when our own purposes are trivial and worthless.

The great Russian writer Tolstoy describes how, after a life of luxury and profligacy, he became at one stage very profoundly dissatisfied and began to search for some meaning in life. First of all, he says, he turned to educated people and thinkers, but he found that they had nothing to offer him except, as he put it, one of the epicurean consolations of life. And he turned instead to the believers among the poor people in Russia, the pilgrims and the monks. He found that though there was a great deal of superstition among them, there was among them a true faith and a reason for living in their teachings. In a very revealing passage,[21] he says:

[21]Stefan Zweig - *Stefan Zweig Presents the Living Thoughts of Tolstoi* – The Living Thoughts Library 3rd Edition 1945.

> 'I understood that I had erred, how I had erred. I had erred not so much through having thought incorrectly as through having lived ill. I understood that the truth had been hidden from me, not so much because I had erred in my reasoning, as because I had led the exceptional life of an epicure bent on satisfying the lusts of the flesh. I understood that my question "what is my life?" and the answer "an evil" were in accordance with the truth of things. The mistake lay in my having applied to life in general an answer which only concerned myself. I had asked what my own life was and the answer was "an evil and an absurdity". Exactly so, my life, a life of indulgence, of sensuality, was an absurdity and an evil. And the answer "life is meaningless and evil" therefore referred only to my own life and not to human life in general. I understood that if I wished to understand life and its meaning, I must live not the life of a parasite but a real life.'

This was a turning point in the life of Tolstoy, and after this he became a real spiritual seeker.

Like Tolstoy and like the three sisters in Chekhov's play, people often ask 'what is the meaning of life?' Our teacher used to say that life was a school or a gymnasium in which we were the pupils. From the empirical point of view we have to give a meaning to life, and we have to give a meaning to our life in order to find out what the real meaning of it is. Perhaps we can agree partly with the existentialists on this point, who hold, as you know, that existence precedes essence; that we merely exist to begin with and that what we become depends on ourselves, upon our conscious choice. We have created what we are, say the Yogis, by our decisions in the past, and we are free to decide now what we shall become. Unless we give a higher purpose to our life, our life will be meaningless and trivial as Tolstoy felt that his was.

As Rousseau said, 'Man is born free and is everywhere in chains.' Well, in his day this was always interpreted politically as being the circumstances of the time. It may well be so, and in places undoubtedly there are still such regimes, but the worst chains from the point of view of the spiritual teachings, say the Yogis, are the chains that man makes by his own choosing. Therefore, one of the teachings of Yoga is that we need to cultivate self-reliance and a sense of purpose if we are to practise Yoga successfully. But not just the self-reliance of the materialist. It is a reliance on the higher Self, on the spiritual element within us, the Lord seated in the hearts of all beings, who promises in the *Gita*: 'To those who turn to Me in faith I provide what they need and protect what they have'.[22]

It is said that Winston Churchill as a young man once said to Violet Bonham Carter: 'All men may be worms but at least I shall be a glow-worm.' Well, this is the right spirit. The aim of the spiritual seeker is not to pretend that he is better than his fellow men, but to contact and manifest the inner source of light, like the glow-worm. To do it we need sincerity and strength of purpose and the right ideal, and if we have these, then nothing will prevent us from succeeding. The aim of Yoga is to strengthen man and to make him independent of circumstances, whereas the worldly life tends to weaken him and to make him dependent on others.

I offer a few more thoughts on this theme, taken from the teachings which Dr Shastri gave to us:

---

[22]*Bhagavad Gita* IX, 22.

> 'The empirical mind operates in the realm of the law of karma. What we sow, we shall reap; what we give, we shall receive hereafter, not necessarily in money but the giving that we give in fellow-feeling or in goodness, and so on. On the other hand, if we create the wrong action, we create conceit, anger, and so on, then we create bonds which bind the Self and do not allow it to fly Godward. We are creating darkness for ourselves and obscuring the inner light.'

There are two main points in this teaching of Yoga. To create the right influences in the mind, to feed the right fuel to the lamp of the mind, we can say is the first point. And secondly, to still the mind in meditation; to still the mind 'like a flame in a windless spot'[23], as the *Gita* says, a flame protected from all disturbing influences, both inner and outer. When the lamp of the mind has had the right fuel and has been protected from all the disturbing influences of desire and aversion, then that flame of thought will be steady, it will be bright, and it will be focussed. Then in meditation, said our teacher, we should take the word 'OM', the symbol of the highest spiritual reality, or, if we prefer it, the word 'Jesus', or any other Avatar, and focus on it in the silenced and stilled mind. We must have silence from the worldly desires and then let the mind swim in the infinity of God within, in peace, beauty and truth. Dr Shastri gave us this meditation:

> 'OM. TRUTH AND BEAUTY ARE THE PROPERTIES OF MY SPIRIT; PEACE AND VIRTUE DROP FROM THE CLOUD OF MY SOUL. OM.'

---

[23] *Bhagavad Gita* VI, 19.

The world offers us many ideals and philosophies but they are mere theories with which to pass the time, and if we play with them, then they leave nothing real behind them. One might say it is like tea tasting. The real tea taster takes a sip of tea and swills it round his mouth, tastes the tea and then he spits it out. He never actually drinks the tea, he only tastes it.

What really matters from the spiritual point of view is something which actually touches our life, which is real, which is not merely an idea, but something we actually put into practice. A little of the meditation practice daily is of more value in giving one a measure of Yoga than any amount of theory. What we should bother about and mind about in life are not the pastimes, but what really affects us, what enables us to realise our inner potentialities. We have to avoid having a closed mind, say the Yogis. Closed minds are dull minds. They are not open to new experiences. All too easily in life we sink into living by clichés, indeed we become almost a living cliché, unless we continually make conscious efforts to learn, to remain open in our minds, to be ready to absorb any new revelation of truth which comes to us.

The Japanese Zen Master Hakuin, who was also a great Yogi, wrote the verse: 'All beings are from the very beginning of the Buddha nature. It is like ice and water; without water no ice can exist.' One of the commentators on this verse says that habits and prejudices in the mind are like freezing. The mind becomes frozen, becomes like ice through our habits and prejudices, through the clichés into which we sink, so to speak, because prejudices and blind habits are like the clichés of the mind. In this mind, which in its raw state is full of prejudices and blind habits, is innately the Buddha nature, the divine nature. You will find water everywhere if you dig deeply enough. A Buddha is an awakened man. What we must do is to try to unfreeze the mind, try to wake up from being overwhelmed by a wrong view.

The aim of Yoga, we can say, is the spiritual awakening of man. Why then do we practise meditation? It is to unfreeze the mind. In order to think clearly, in order to see clearly, in order to awaken the inner light, we have to remove the darkness, we have to remove the obscurity. It means, among other things, says the great modern Yogi, Swami Rama Tirtha, the denial of the interests of the little ego and the assertion of the real Self of man, the assertion of the spiritual nature of man. This ego has acquisitive power-loving propensities. But the mind also has the higher urges, the idealistic urges, the self-transcending urges. Within the mind, self-assertion and self-abasement are only two sides of the same medal. What really matters is self-transcendence, to widen the view of life, to awaken the inner light.

Einstein once said: 'I believe in a spiritual force behind the universe but not one that cares a jot for the fate of the individual.' Well, we are not saying that this is the same view as the yogic doctrine. But here there is a sense in Einstein, a sense that there is a spiritual reality behind the universe, and it is something which cuts across the interests of the ego. It represents the higher Self of man, the higher interests of man. If we ask a contemporary Western man-in-the-street what he thinks the nature of man is, then he regards man only as a combination of the mind and the body and he thinks, no doubt, that when we understand all about these two, all about the mind and all about the body, then we shall know all there is to know about man. Well, we can agree that the brain is the organ of mind, and we can agree that the mechanism of this organ is ill understood but that we understand much more of it than we used to. The point is very important. Even to understand fully how the brain works, even to understand fully the physiology of the body, is not to understand how to live well. You may fully understand how a grand piano works but that does not mean that you can play it. Indeed those who can play it, probably understand very little about it. Say that you went, for instance, to Schnabel, the pianist. Probably he would have understood very little of the physics involved in the ballistic action of the hammers, but he was better than anybody else in using that action, at making the hammers hit the keys to produce the exact tone and the exact sound that he wanted.

So to understand something in the scientific sense is not at all the same as understanding how to use that thing. To understand even the mind is not the same as knowing how to use it well. We want to know how to use the mind well, not only how it works. Because knowing how to use it, we know how to create harmony and light and beauty, not only for ourselves but for others also. We can say that all the problems that surround us in the modern world, the problem of war, the problem of totalitarianism, the problem of social and domestic strife and unhappiness, are all ultimately the outcome of the maladjusted human mind, of our inability, collectively and individually, to use the mind well. So this subject is one of the greatest importance.

I leave you with a verse from another Japanese Zen master. It expresses the same thought which was hinted at in the verse by Hakuin, that the spiritual nature of man is something which is already there, is already present within the mind of man, that this inner light is obscured by the darkness of the mind, and in order that it shall be known and shall manifest its power, we have to awaken the mind to this inner light. This is the verse: 'The fish in the middle of the water does not know the water although born and brought up and living in the water.' A man in the midst of the spiritual reality does not know that reality.

4

THE PRACTICE OF RECOLLECTION*

WHAT IS IT which marks out an athlete from an ordinary man? Both alike clearly use the physical body and both undertake physical activity of many different kinds. But one can say that the ordinary man's activity is in a sense haphazard, undirected and semi-unconscious. It's done, in other words, wherever by chance it becomes necessary in order to achieve other ends. The activity is incidental to the other purposes of the ordinary man. Frequently it is aimless and it is very often inefficient and vacillating. As compared with this, any serious athlete trains systematically and consciously. He has a quite different attitude, at least as regards his training, towards the body and its physical activity. He controls it and he also develops the body. He does it with a very definite aim in view: to achieve much greater feats, physically speaking, than the body was previously capable of.

Now Yoga is exactly like the training of an athlete in one sense, not in regard to the body, but in regard to the mind. Both the Yogi and the ordinary man certainly use their minds and they use their minds in many different activities. But the activity is nonetheless different in the two cases and the attitude towards the activity is different. The Yogi aims to use his mind consciously and he systematically trains his mental activity so that the mind will obey him. Now, of

---

*A lecture given on 5th December 1969.

course, no athlete trains for twenty-four hours in the day, nor even throughout his waking hours, and in the same way no Yogi undertakes formal mental training for the whole of the day. Both the athlete and the Yogi have formal periods when the training is undertaken. But again, although this is true and although these periods may be relatively short periods during the day, both of them go on exercising some control over their activity – in the case of the athlete, the activity of the body, in the case of the Yogi, the activity of the mind – at times other than the formal training practice periods. There is a certain discipline, one can say, present at all times in those undergoing the training. And this is certainly true in the case of the mental training of the Yogi.

Like the athlete, the Yogi undertakes the training, not for its own sake but in order to acquire skill; skill in using his mind for a definite end. He wants to train for a definite achievement and that achievement is the successful undertaking of the enquiry into his own nature. This is not a mere theoretical enquiry but it is a practical task aimed to give him mastery of his instruments – the body and the mind – and freedom from the limitations which they impose on him in their present state. There is a great distinction between training and theory about training.

To take a specific instance in the athletic field – if you think of a cricketer, the skill of a cricketer, one can say that an expert cricketer knows, actually knows in a real sense, exactly how to throw the ball and to catch it, how to hit it where he wants to. He also knows in practice what putting a particular spin on the ball will do to make the ball bounce regularly. He actually knows this in a real sense, and the sense in which it is known is that he has experience of it and can actually use it to predict what will be the result of certain movements and tactics which he undertakes. He can use this knowledge in practice to do what he wants to a great extent. It's equally true, however, that the cricketer may not even be able to understand when a physicist explains to him the dynamics of moving objects or the mathematics, for instance, of the transfer of the momentum from his bat to the ball. And this is not a very advanced part of dynamics, as those who have studied physics know. Many cricketers would surely be completely bemused by such explanations. Nowadays people often conclude in a simple-minded way that the cricketer is an ignorant man and that the physicist is a clever one, yet it is more than likely that the physicist, if you put him on the cricket field, would be unable to catch the ball or to hit it for one, let alone for six. It is worth reminding ourselves of this, because the same principle holds for any skill. There are very few people who can play the violin like Heifetz or the piano like Schnabel; many more might give an expert explanation of the theory of piano playing or the physical principles involved.

Yoga, then, is a training for practice, like the training of the athlete or the cricketer, and not a training for theory. It is not really concerned with the theoretical study of psychology or physiology except, and only except, where these are relevant to the practical training. It is concerned with acquiring the skill of using the mind, using it well in practical life, and also acquiring it with a view to achieving what can be achieved in this sphere: a knowledge of the real Self of man.

In any training one can say there are two phases: the preparation and the practice itself. Just as an athlete starts by getting himself into shape, as he says, and limbering up before going to the actual practice of the skill or the event or the game with which he is concerned, so the task of the Yogi is to start working on his mind as the very first step in Yoga. In one sense, one can say it is like limbering it up before any formal practice of the path of Yoga begins. Now the activity for which the Yogi has to prepare himself is laid down in the Yoga classics and it is *vichara*, enquiry. The preparatory stages, of which the masters of Yoga tell us, have to be undertaken before this, so to speak, limbering up. Finding out how to use the mind, preparing it for the task, is spoken of by the Yogis as the acquisition of the necessary qualifications for that task of enquiry. It is said that there are two such essential qualifications: firstly, the control and restraint of the mind, in other words, bringing the mental functions under the conscious control of the will; and the second qualification is the purification of the mind.

We are used to the fact that in any skill in ordinary life there are different schools of training, and they often grow up independently in different parts of the world. The detail of the training may be different from place to place. A good example of this is singing. The methods of training used, for instance, in the Viennese and the German schools of singing are different in detail from the methods used in Britain or, again, from the methods used in Russia and the Slavonic countries. But one can say that all the schools which are concerned with a particular skill, with teaching people to acquire a particular skill, must meet and solve the same basic problems. In singing, for instance, one has got to solve the problems of breath control and of sound production. One has the same potential defects to meet, like excessive wobbling on the note. It is well known that some methods of training are not as good as others at avoiding this. However, one can say that, on the whole, even though these schools grow up independently and in quite different places, because they are dealing with the same skill and they have the same problems to meet, there will be more in common between them than there will be dissimilarities.

We can say that exactly the same is true of the mystics. If we examine what the Western mystics have said, there is, of course, unfortunately little enough formal record in the West of the methods employed. This is the great difference between Indian mysticism, for instance, and the Western mystics. We have very little formal record of the training and the methods used in this part of the world. However, if we compare the Western mystics with the Eastern, we find the same basic ingredients of the training spoken of using other terms. We find that the same two qualifications, the same two preparatory requisites, the same two limbering up practices, so to speak, are spoken of by the Western mystics. They are called by the Western mystics recollection and purgation. They are exactly the same practices. This recollection is the restraint and control of the functions of the mind. It does not mean what we commonly mean by recollection, namely remembering something. This is a technical term used by the Western mystics. Purgation means, of course, the purification of the mind. The Western mystics speak of the process to which these are preparatory: the process of enquiry leading to enlightenment or knowledge, illumination.

Let us say something, then, of the first step in this path of Yoga, called in the East the control and restraint of the mind and in the West the practice of recollection. Perhaps the most characteristic thing about the mind, about anyone's mind, is its ability to rapidly shift its focus of attention. The eye has a fixation point at which its vision is most acute. The grain of the resolution of the vision is much finer at the fixation point of the eye than it is in the periphery. At least in daylight this is certainly true, and the eye is rotated, seeing things this way and that, and the head is also moved so that whatever we catch sight of and want to look at, is focussed on this particular point on the retina. It might not have been so – we might simply have had a uniform sense organ which was equally good at seeing things anywhere, and equally bad, of course, and we simply scanned the whole field. But it isn't so. The whole mechanism of the eye, the movements of the eye in the head, and also the control of the movements of the neck, which are very intimately connected in the nervous system with the eyes, in the fixation, is so arranged that wherever we are, whatever catches our attention and whatever we want to look at, we can move the eyes so that this area of most acute vision round the fixation point can be brought to bear on the object and the image of the object can be focussed there by the lens of the eye.

Just as in the eye there is one area where we fixate, where we have a fixation point and our vision is best there, so the mind too has a focus of attention. It is likened in the Sanskrit classics on Yoga to the moving point of an arrow. Of course, many of these yogic classics were written thousands of years ago and they had to use the analogies which were familiar and which were available to them. They likened it to the moving point of an arrow which was directed towards the sensation or object or thought which caught the interest, which partook in the perception of the object, which allowed the object to be perceived. This focus of attention in the mind can switch rapidly from one thing to another and it can also be heightened and lowered. The more intense it is, the more unaware we shall be of the objects or ideas which occupy the fringe of our consciousness.

If you liken the mind to a stage, then one might say that the focus of attention is like the spotlight focussed on the star performer of the moment. The intensity of the attention might be likened to the ratio of the brightness of the spotlight to that of the surrounding stage. But I think in many ways the stage is not such a good analogy as the television screen. The information reaching the mind from the senses comes from quite a long way away from the mind through the nerves and it has already undergone a great deal of transformation before it gets to consciousness. The mind, as you know, like the television screen, is capable of producing illusions quite as remarkable as the TV engineers can produce. You can very well believe this when you consider the heightened sensory illusions which are produced by mescaline and other drugs.

Moreover, when one thinks of TV and the TV programme, what appears on the screen isn't simply a picture of what is happening in front of all the cameras which are on; something is chosen from one of the cameras. The director, who is unseen, chooses which camera he is going to use at any moment and he also directs where it is to be pointed and whether it is to do a close-up or a long distance shot or to move, and then he can switch from one to the other. In the same way, in the mind what is presented in the focus of attention in consciousness can be any of the inputs from any of the senses. What we don't attend to, what has not caught our attention, particularly if we are attending intensely to something else, can be completely missed although the senses are recording passively this event.

In the Yoga classics a simile is given of a smith at his work, making an arrowhead in front of his shop in the street, concentrating very intensely on beating the tip of the arrow as the procession of a king goes by down the street. When he is asked afterwards what he thought of the procession, he says: 'What procession?' Because he was concentrating so intensely on the job in hand, his attention was given to his task and he hadn't noticed what was going on. Well this, you may say, is just a story but there are many such instances of intense concentration.

A writer, I think it was Romain Rolland, describes how at the studio of Rodin one evening, Rodin had him and another friend to dinner and after dinner the artist who was feeling very genial said, 'Would you like to come into the studio and I'll show you the work that I am at the moment engaged on?' This was a great privilege; usually he didn't like people seeing his things when they were on their way. They were taken in and they saw this figure that Rodin was sculpting. He was showing it to them and talking to them for a bit about it; then he suddenly looked at the figure and he said 'Can you excuse me for just a minute?' He had seen something and he took up the chisel, went over to the figure, and began to correct something which he thought was wrong. For the next two hours they stood there and watched, and he seemed to be completely unconscious of anything else but the figure. They were so impressed, they thought this was such a wonderful experience to see him working, that they were quite happy to stand there and watch this going on. This is another example from real life of intense attention, intense concentration, and how it cuts out any other input.

There are many other examples that one can give. One other perhaps is worth mentioning. The Russian physiologist Pavlov was taken by his wife to a performance of *La Bohème* in Moscow, at the Bolshoi. He was asked next day by one of his colleagues in the laboratory how he enjoyed it, because it was not very often that he went to the theatre. He said, 'Well, I'm sorry but I was so intensely thinking about a problem I am working on at the moment, that I really didn't notice anything that was going on on the stage!'

This is a state of mind, then, that occurs even in ordinary life of one-pointed attention, a state which the Yogis call *ekagra*, the one-pointed mind. It is an unusual state and it is only achieved, one can say, by intense interest and by long practice, whether that practice is conscious or unconscious. It's like the feat of a fully trained athlete. It's like excelling, if you like, in the high jump or the long jump after long training. Whether that training has been undertaken consciously or unconsciously, it's only the really trained man who can achieve this one-pointedness, through long practice of the mind in concentration. Much more commonly the mind is not in the state of *ekagra*, of one-pointedness, but in one of its other states which the Yogis call *mudha* (dull) or *kshipta* (fickle). The dull state which the Yogis describe shows that there is a great difference between intense one-pointed concentration on something and simply not attending to anything at all.

The mind sometimes gets into a lazy, stuporous condition in which it hardly attends to anything and you might well suppose it's like Rodin, absolutely unaware of anything that is going on around. I have been in that state many times. But it is not; it is quite a different state. It is the state which the Yogis call *mudha*, not a manifestation of skilful control of the mind and restraint but a manifestation of apathy. More commonly perhaps we know the mind, or we recognise the mind, when it is in an active and energetic state. Then the attention is active, we are attending to things, but it is, so to speak, free running, flitting to and fro, this way and that, without any real aim or direction, and this is what the Yogis call the fickle state of the mind. It is the unproductive grasshopper state of the mind, which the *Bhagavad Gita* and the *Upanishads* speak of when they say, 'The mind of the irresolute is many-branched

[24] *Bhagavad Gita* II, 41.

and endless.'[24] They say of it that in this mind, the mind in this state, the focus of attention can be swept away at a moment's notice, either by something impinging on the senses or by the winds of passion or prejudice arising from the unconscious.

If you want to see one manifestation of this aspect of the mind, objectified in behaviour, I suppose a good example is the behaviour of a spoilt child. It wants attention the whole time; it doesn't want to sustain anything; it continually wants something different and yet it is most unsatisfied. Mind you, the child can be of any age. Chekhov in *Uncle Vanya* has drawn an excellent picture of the mind in this state in the old Moscow professor who comes to stay. He thinks he is the great man of the family, he visits his poor country cousins, and he expects the whole of the house to dance attendance on him. He is really a volcano of inflated egoity. He is hypochondriacal and there is the wonderful scene which Chekhov writes in the middle act of *Uncle Vanya* where he oscillates between hypochondriacal ruminations. He first wants the window open, then he wants it closed; he wants people to bring him things; he is jealous of his younger wife and so on – a very good picture of a spoilt child in old age. This is one example of the fickle state of the mind of which the Yogis speak, the unrestrained and uncontrolled mind.

The first step in Yoga practice, then, is the control and restraint of the mind. It can be likened to the first painful session of limbering up by someone who has taken far too little exercise for far too long, who suddenly decides that they have got to get fit. As with people in this situation, unfortunately it is those who most need it who are least likely to take it up.

In the Western tradition Evelyn Underhill says, the

practice of recollection (the Western name for this stage) is no more than the subjection of the attention to the control of the will. It is a gradual process which begins with the deliberate and regular practice of meditation. She quotes St Theresa's words to her pupils, who are beginning meditation, where she says: 'I do not require of you to form great and curious considerations in your understanding. I require of you no more than to look.' Recollection, the subjection of the attention to the control of the will, enables one to look. For it is only when one can attend to something with a steadily focussed and undistracted gaze that one really begins to see what is there. But initially the steady vision is not the explicit object of the practice. It is the control of the wayward mind that is required so that it can be rendered one-pointed. Until the athlete has limbered up and got into training, he cannot really begin to practise effectively the game which he intends to perfect. And until the Yogi has got control of the faculties of his mind and can restrain it, he isn't really in a situation where he can undertake the enquiry, the *vichara*, which is the main subject of Yoga.

Meditation, then, is a practice *par excellence* which leads to this control, the training practice. In the initial stages of the meditation the particular text or symbol or thought that one takes for the meditation is not so important. It's better to take one of the traditional texts, many of which are given by our teacher, Dr Hari Prasad Shastri, for instance, in his book on meditation,[25] which you can yourself practise. The actual choice of the text can be made at will because this is not the main concern of the initial stage of this practice. The main thing is that, once one has made the choice, one must hold and defend that choice in the focus

---

[25] Hari Prasad Shastri, *Meditation – its Theory and Practice,* Shanti Sadan, 1936.

of attention during the meditation period. And to hold and defend it involves struggle. It is, say the mystics, a kind of beginning of the spiritual warfare because there will be many invasions from outside; there will be many insidious encroachments of other things into the mind; there may be even very spiritual thoughts which come. If you give way to them and you don't continue to focus on the meditation that you have chosen, then you are not practising the meditation as it should be practised.

One should also, in starting meditation, decide how long one will meditate and stick to that time. One might suppose, how wonderful, if one is doing well one can go on indefinitely; if one is doing badly, well, I'll do a little bit and then stop. But this is to defeat the main object of the meditation in the early phase, which is the subjection of the attention to the control of the will, to decide what the focus of the meditation will be beforehand, to decide the time for which one will meditate, and then to stick to that. There are many distractions that will come but one must continually return the mind to focus on the object of the meditation. At times, as many of the mystics have said of the beginning of meditation, one gets a restless boredom arising in the mind.

A dreary conviction of your own incapacity will presently attack you, Evelyn Underhill says. And this too must be resisted at the sword point. Never before, the meditator finds, has the stream flowed so slowly or fifteen minutes taken so long to pass. Anyone who has tried meditation has had these experiences at the beginning and the success of doing this is the same as the success of the athlete who decides to limber up and doesn't stop when he feels stiff or cold or it's not a nice day.

'Abandoning all desires born of imagination,'[26] says

[26]*Bhagavad Gita* VI, 24, 25 and 27.

the *Gita*, 'and turning the senses from their objects by the power of the mind, let the aspirant slowly, patiently, with the higher mind fixed on the Self attain the great peace.' He must not waste his mind force by dwelling on outer objects. The restless wavering mind tries to get away from the Self before the Self is fully realised. The Yogi must curb the activities of the mind and focus it again and again on the Self. Like a flame sheltered from the wind the mind of a Yogi, subdued and focussed on the Self, does not waver.

Swami Rama Tirtha says that at this stage of the Yoga, the Yogi is like Majnun, the traditional lover of the Sufi literature in Persia. The story is that he wanted to journey to see his beloved Leila who lived in a town at the other side of the desert. In order to get there he had to travel by camel. He got a she-camel but, although he didn't know it, the she-camel had just had a foal and her young foal was in the town which they were leaving. Majnun started out across the desert, and every time that in the hot sun he began to nod and to go to sleep, the she-camel would turn round and go back to the place where they had just come from. He would wake again, realise what had happened, and turn round. In this way, it is said, a two days' journey lasted many months. Well, this is a story but you can see the application of the story. The she-camel, of course, is the mind which, like the unfit man, wanting to train for the athletics, has been allowed to have its own way and, through long practice of indulging itself as it wants, is very difficult to bring under control. It is, as the mystics all agree, a slow and gradual process by which this restraint and control of the mind has to be achieved.

The mind, says the *Gita*, is like a lamp: when fickle and distracted, the flame flickers and it gives no steady light. It is the sheltered and concentrated mind, shielded from the winds of passion and self-indulgence, that produces the steady flame. Then, as well as recollection, as well as the restraint and control of the mind, there is the second qualification of which the Yogis speak: the purification of the mind. If the flame of the lamp is to be clear and bright, then the fuel in the lamp must be pure. Otherwise one will only get a smoky flame which gives only a dim and ineffective light. The fuel must be pure and the wick must be cleaned and trimmed. Meditation, the practice of recollection, the restraint and control of the functions of the mind in meditation, leads to the steady flame, the control of attention, the control of the focus of attention in the mind. But to achieve also a clear flame we cannot ignore, say the Yogis, the ethical discipline. The mind must not be engaged deeply in the trivial or the degrading because it takes on the quality of that which it attends to deeply or with interest. As far as possible, we should universalise our goodwill and not wish ill to anyone. And we should avoid those great impurities in the mind: anger, greed and lust. The *Katha Upanishad* says: ‘This Self cannot be reached through right knowledge by one who has not desisted from evil ways, nor by him who is not tranquil, nor by him who has not a concentrated mind, nor even by one whose mind is not restrained and stilled.’ In this way, when the mind has desisted from evil ways, when it is tranquil, when it is concentrated, and when it is restrained and stilled, then it is rendered fit to undertake the enquiry and to achieve the spiritual knowledge.

Swami Rama Tirtha says: ‘God is nearer to thee than the jugular vein. When thy inner eyes are opened, thou wilt cry “Allah is”, “Allah is”; “I am God” will be thy triumphant cry. Remember God is nearer to thee than the jugular vein.’ It is the teaching of the Yogis that the real Self of man is divine. We are like the fish in water, says the Japanese sage Muso Kokushi;[27] although we live and move and have our being in the water, we don't know of the existence of the water because we can never get outside the water and look at it and say: 'Ah yes, so that's water.' It isn't a doctrine of pantheism. It isn't a doctrine that everything in the world is spiritual, because the reality is an inner reality. The empirical world has an empirical existence but it doesn't have a transcendental reality, a spiritual reality, say the Yogis. As the *Gita* says in chapter thirteen: 'Beyond and yet within all beings, whether moving or unmoving, that reality is so subtle that it is incomprehensible to the intellect. It is both near and far.'[28] It is indefinable in words and yet it has a practical validity and it can be directly experienced.

There are some very wise words by Albert Einstein when he said: 'We must recognise that what is impenetrable to us exists and is the source of the highest wisdom and the most radiant beauty.' This is one of the greatest intellects of our time, of this century, speaking. To the intellect it is an impenetrable reality. It is impenetrable to us, he says, but even so, we must recognise that it exists and that it is the source of the highest wisdom and the most radiant beauty. Yoga, on the other hand, says that as the basis of the mind, that which is behind the mind, can be directly and consciously realised by man. And the reason for practising the restraint and control of the mind in Yoga is with a view to knowing this truth.

The enlightenment of the Yogis isn't intellectual knowledge. It isn't like the knowledge of the physicist

---

[27]This teacher is also known as Muso Seseki. Muso Kokushi (1275–1351) is the author of *Dream Conversations on Buddhism and Zen,* translated by Thomas Cleary, 31 August 1996.

[28]*Bhagavad Gita* XIII, 15.

of the physics of cricket. It is a direct experience, say the Yogis, *anubhava,* and it comes suddenly. Plato in our own Western tradition speaks of it when he says, 'This kind of knowledge is a thing that comes in a moment, like a light kindled from a leaping spark which, once it has reached the soul, finds its own fuel.' It comes in a moment like a light kindled from a leaping spark, but once attained, say the Yogis, it lasts for ever and it leads to the state which is called in the *Gita 'sthita prajna'*, the state of the man established in wisdom.

I end with a verse from the Chinese tradition which describes this end of Yoga:[29]

> 'Unexpectedly the path comes to an end.
> When stamped through the waves were only water.
> They say that the old Master Chao Chu stands supremely above the rest.
> But nothing extraordinary I find in his features.'

[29]It's not known if this is the source of this quote but it appears to be commonly used and ancient. See, Daisetz Teitaro Suzuki, *The Zen Koan as a means of Attaining Enlightenment,* the work was originally published by Ricker and Company in 1950 in *Essays in Zen Buddhism,* second series edited by Christmas Humphries.

5

The Unitive Life*

WE ALL KNOW people who always miss the point of anything they are told. They fail to see jokes, don't grasp the significance of even the most obvious events and generally provide their fellow creatures with endless causes of mirth or exasperation. They bumble along through life making a mess of everything like the proverbial bull in the china shop and, though ignorance is said to be bliss, no sensible person envies them. And yet, if the spiritual teachers are right, we are all in our own ways equally obtuse over many things. Because we miss the point time and again in our dealings with friends and acquaintances, in our life at work or at home, we are continually stumbling over personalities and hurting both ourselves and others, stubbing the sensitive toe of our ego against some unusually hard object resisting its progress.

It is about this that the spiritual teachers come to speak to us, with something to say which is immediately practical and important and which has a bearing on our own present happiness or misery. They do not seek to impose on us any far-off theory or theoretical doctrine or abstract principle. They talk to us of enlightenment because, as Swami Rama Tirtha says: 'The man working without self-knowledge is like a person working in a darkened room, knocking his head against the wall, banging his knee against

*A lecture given on 1st February 1961.

the table, tumbling over chairs and receiving all sorts of bumps and blows.' It is only when he has ushered light into the room that he can work without a struggle.

We are like the man who knows that a horse can help one to get from place to place, but has never learnt how to control it. Instead of riding the horse of our mind, we catch hold of its tail in the hope that it will drag us along and we are surprised when we get nothing but kicks from it. But this is not the horse's fault, but ours! Only when we mount it and tame it and use it, as a steed should be used, will our mind become a real instrument of knowledge for us. A Sufi verse says: 'The body and mind are the camel which can take a man to the *Kaaba* of enlightenment [the *Kaaba* is the object of pilgrimage at Mecca]. If you do not go on this pilgrimage it is not because you have no ass, but because you are one!'

How is it then that we miss the point? We miss it, say the Yogis, because our knowledge is inadequate. Those of you who have had the misfortune to have to sit for an examination ill-prepared may know that there is no greater misery than not knowing your stuff. I had to sit many such examinations and had a chance to test this for myself. The exams which you forgot about until four nights before, when a sudden terror seized you and you then mugged up five or ten spot questions in the hope that some of the right ones would come up, were a great example of how not to do things, because you went into the exam already half defeated. Your knowledge was totally inadequate and you knew it to be so, and if you got away with it, then it was with little satisfaction. Anything out of the ordinary spelt failure and even things one found out one knew about afterwards were often missed, because of the lack of confidence that one's ignorance entailed.

Most of us go through the examination of life in the same lamentable condition, trusting to luck that only the few questions we feel we can answer will come up. We are always wrong! Sooner or later some of the questions to which we don't know the appropriate response present themselves and the result once more is that we miss the point. Of course, it is not meant here that, as in the school or university examination, what we lack is a store of mugged-up facts, but that we lack the much more important insight or enlightenment of which the Yogis and mystics speak, that insight which lets us respond rightly to events and allows us to see into the hearts and minds of others.

The secret is the state of our mind. The mind is the instrument of our knowledge, our 'organ of experience', as the Yogis call it, and upon its state depends our weal or woe. It is not simply a recorder of experience like a camera; it is an active participator, always interpreting, transforming and attending or not attending. It is intensely active as a participator, a moulder of experience, and not passive like the wax in the hands of Madame Tussaud. It is an instrument capable of colossal errors and missing the point; its self-delusions and its misinterpretations can be terrible and destructive. In the mind of Othello, played on by the crafty Iago, the unbridled delusions of jealousy destroyed not only what he loved but himself too. In a Macbeth or a Richard III the warping influence of devilish ambition, destroying the moral sense, led to murder and disillusionment. In the stupidity and self-indulgence of a Lear, the mind's love of flattery made him completely miss the true character of the people with whom he was dealing and led to the downfall of a great king. We all know too well what we have suffered in recent history from the mad delusions of the mind of a Hitler.

What, then, is to be done about this instrument of the mind which is subject to so many maladies and defects? The masters of Yoga reply: 'Don't depend on it entirely, rule it and don't make it your master. Ride the mind, don't be dragged along by the mind.' There is an old Chinese verse:[30]

> 'Hundreds of spring flowers, the autumnal moon,
> The refreshing summer breeze, winter snow;
> Free thy mind from idle thoughts
> And for thee how enjoyable is every season.'

It is the misinterpretations of the mind, its idle thoughts, which make us not only miss the point but are a cause of great unhappiness because they distort our picture of things as they are.

How easily we jump to conclusions, and how much easier if those conclusions are damaging to others. Ask any cheap journalist of the relative news value of a good deed and a bad one. Why? Because it enhances our own feeling of superiority. Criticism you will very easily get from others, appreciation is a much rarer commodity. As the *Upanishad* says: 'Those who do not purify their minds and seek enlightenment only waste their time and speak ill of others.'

Our teacher used to tell a story of an old man who went on a journey with his son and his ass. Being old, he rode on the ass while his son walked by his side. But as they passed through the first village they heard the people saying: 'What a selfish old man riding the ass the whole time while that poor boy has to walk!' The old man was rather sensitive, so before they came to the next village he got off and let his son ride and they heard the people saying as they went through: 'Look at that for the modern generation! A

[30]Verse by Mumon (Wumen) who was a Chinese Chan Master (1183–1260), in D T Suzuki, *Essays in Zen Buddhism.*

healthy strapping boy riding while his poor old father has to walk beside him!' At the next village they both got on the ass and the people said: 'It's inhuman, expecting that ass to carry both men; it shouldn't be allowed! What brutes they are!' At the fourth village they both walked and led the ass and the people said: 'Look at that pair – they must be daft; they have a perfectly good ass and they both walk!'

To work for a great name, or to acquire a reputation, is likely to be equally frustrating, and if the reputation comes, it is more likely to come to the man who has never given it a thought than to the ambitious politician who tries to ingratiate himself with the crowd. And even if reputation is achieved, it is fragmentary and can change or vanish in a moment. He who is waiting for universal appreciation in this world must have either the optimism of a Micawber or expect to live as long as Methuselah.

The first thing that we have to learn from Yoga is that the mind is changeable. Its present state is not its only state and not its ultimate state. The mind has to be refined and brought into contact with the region of transcendence. Until it is, we shall be like the man who sees the bent stick in water and thinks that it is really bent. All through life we shall miss the point because we shall interpret wrongly what the world is like.

Religion and the spiritual teachings are nothing extra, nothing added to ordinary life. They are the fulfilment of ordinary life, the rendering, perfect and whole, of the personality, and something more, the realisation of the springs of the personality in the region of transcendence. Our ambition is the result of a misunderstanding, our pride is the result of a misunderstanding, our selfishness is the result of a misunderstanding of ourselves and the world, and is not something which can be quickly and easily corrected, nor can it be corrected by the application of force of any kind. It can only be rectified by a new and deeper understanding, by knowledge.

There is a story that a scientist got the curly tail of a dog and straightened it by sealing it for fifteen years in a straight tube, but when he removed the dog's tail from the tube it simply curled up again. In the same way, any outer coercion or force applied to the personality, whether of will or austerity, will not readily alter its aberrations in the long run. Only one thing will do so: a new vision, an inner enlightenment.

First, we have to know what is possible, that the mind is teachable, that the present phase of life is only a preparation for a deeper phase of life, that the present life of the mind is only a preparation for a higher and profounder life and it lies in our power to bring this about. At the moment we are like the men living in a cave of whom Plato speaks in the seventh book of his *Republic*. We live only in the shadows, but we have to come out into the light to see things as they really are. So long as the mind is unenlightened, even if we do make achievements, it is often without truly realising their significance.

Christopher Columbus is revered as the man who discovered America, but if you study the life of Columbus, you find that he himself dreamed only of gold and wealth. There are still copies of many of the books of earlier voyages, which he read before he set out on his great voyage and in them, in his own hand, any passage which speaks of gold or treasure being rumoured in distant lands is marked. His great dream was to find a new route to the riches of the spice trade, a new route to the East Indies, and he died thinking that he had done so with no idea of the Pacific between the land he had found and his imagined goal.

So the achievements of the unpurified mind cannot be relied upon and are seldom recognised by that mind itself. In the Zen ox-herding pictures, the first step in the training is depicted as recognising the existence of the mind, finding the mind, because only when its existence as an instrument and its nature have been recognised, can it be trained.

The yogic doctrine denies emphatically the idea which one finds in Freudian psychology that man is necessarily at the mercy of his mind. It shows that he is only at the mercy of it if he has not bothered to learn about it, train it and discipline it into a useful servant. Because, like all the spiritual teachers, the Yogis show emphatically that the mind is teachable and that man is master of his own fate, and to make their point more challengingly, it is from those, whom the wisdom of the world, the considered judgement of the social scientist and the psychological expert, dismiss as inferior types, that the spiritual teachers have so often found their greatest followers. What would a selection committee have made of the twelve fishermen of Galilee whom Jesus turned into world teachers? Or of the boy Hastamalaka, considered by his community what would now be called 'educationally subnormal', who became one of the four great pillars of Shri Shankara? And the spiritual teachers have always maintained that no stone can be rejected for each has within it the potentiality of becoming the headstone in the corner.

The potentialities of each and every man are infinite from the spiritual point of view because in each there is a divine element, asleep as yet in most, but which can be awakened by the traditional methods. Like the power in the nucleus of the atom, the spiritual power lies hidden in the heart of man, but it may wait a thousand years before it is awakened, and it will only be awakened when its existence is recognised and the life of the individual turns towards it. This is what is spoken of as restoring man to his nature, or as the Zen people say, seeing the 'original face', the face that each man had before his mother and father were born. But the point is that it is nothing unnatural to man; it is the most supremely natural thing about him. For the discovery of the follower of Yoga in his ascent on the path, is that everything else which seemed to be his nature turns out in the end to have been only a borrowed glory, only another coat covering the real Self within.

Science may speak of evolution but the spiritual teachers have spoken of evolution long before. In the twelfth century, Maulana Rumi gives a detailed account of the progress of the soul of the individual through the state of rocks where consciousness abides in the deep sleep of the inanimate world, stirring in the plants, dreaming in animals and awakening to full self-consciousness in man. But, says Rumi, this is not the final stage – man has to progress yet further to transcend the ordinary human consciousness and touch the transcendent consciousness of the spiritual realm.

One of the doctrines well known to biologists is that, to give it in ponderous scientific jargon, 'ontogeny recapitulates phylogeny', which means simply that the development of each individual in its own life repeats, so to say in a condensed and immensely speeded-up way, the development of the whole animal kingdom from which it has evolved. Thus, at a certain stage in development even the human embryo has gills like a fish and shares many of the features of the amphibia and other lower creatures which are subsequently lost. We carry our history with us, both our own history and the history of the whole of humanity, indeed of the whole living kingdom, and much of what we find ourselves with is a vestige of that earlier stage in our development, like that tiresome organ, the appendix. Many of the passions and instincts of the lower mind are still remnants of man's animal origins. But whereas in the animal they are natural and necessary, in man they are only taking their rightful place if they become subservient to the higher functions of the mind, the more highly evolved faculties of reason and intuition which make man Homo sapiens. If we become ruled by the animal side of our nature, we have regressed in evolution as much as if we had returned to an animal incarnation.

What the Yogis tell us is that each individual can live on any plane of his being – the sensual, the emotional, the rational, the intuitive, the aesthetic or the spiritual – but as man we must choose to live on the highest. Only then will the lower faculties take their rightful place in the body politic. Life in the organism is a kind of hierarchy in which the simplest and the most primitive are retained to serve as the groundwork for the more evolved finer and subtler functions. Those of you who read the classic of the great physiologist, Sir Charles Sherrington, *The Integrative Action of the Nervous System*, will know how he demonstrates that the highest functions of the nervous system are built up step-by-step on the simplest groundwork of the most primitive automatic reflexes. The less evolved serves as the essential groundwork to the more evolved but, as Aristotle says, the whole is greater than the sum of these parts. Real freedom for the individual is to take one's stand on the highest plane of man's being and on something beyond the highest plane, the region of transcendence, the divine element, called the Self (*Atman*) by the Yogis, not by killing the lower but by letting it take its proper place in service of the higher.

To live on one of the lower planes is not out of place at a certain stage in man's evolution and development. But the aim of Yoga is to restore man to his real nature, to his transcendent nature. What the Yogis mean was well said by a great English mystic of the seventeenth century, Isaac Pennington. If we celebrate the Lord Mayor's Show in London for no other reason, we should celebrate the fact that a Lord Mayor of London was the father of this great English mystic. He expressed a profound spiritual truth when he wrote: 'There is no truth except the last, except the uttermost, yet everything is true in its own part, which is shadow from an intenser substance.'

It is a little like the doctrine of F. H. Bradley, that in partial revelation of truth in its absolute form in the world of phenomenal appearance there are degrees of truth, which we can arrange in a sequence, each revealing a more comprehensive picture of reality than what went before. Man's idea of himself goes through the same evolution. He lives identified first only with the body and the senses, then with his feelings, then with his will and reason, but beyond this is the inspired vision of the artist and beyond even this, the knowledge of himself as he really is, as a spiritual being.

How is this process to be carried out? By consciously directing the mind, by withdrawing it from unnecessary interest in outer distractions. We are continually having invitations to dissipate our energies in this way and that. Like investors in the Stock Exchange, we are besieged by share-pushers anxious to unload their shares on us in return for the capital of our time and mental energy. But we must ask very carefully, before we accept these offers, what guaranteed interest rates we can expect, what returns will the investment bring, not only in short-term enjoyment, but in long-term satisfaction? All too often the concerns in which we invest our mental capital burst and evaporate like the South Sea Bubble and we are left the poorer.

So the first two things to be done, say the Yogis, are to make a definite resolution to take the mind in hand, not by coercion but by persuasion and gentle persistence, and to direct our mental energies and interests along those channels which will elevate the mind and enrich it, and not leave it bankrupt and depleted.

The senses are like Turkish tailors. Customers take their own cloth to be made up. The tailors tell amazing stories and while you are laughing they snip and steal more and more away. The senses snip away at our life.

I offer you a practice which our teacher, Dr Shastri, gave so that those of you who wish to try it, may do it for yourselves. If you do it for three weeks to a month you will be able to see for yourself the difference in the mind which it creates. Sit quietly and take a few deep breaths to still the mind, then decide to concentrate your mind for the next five to ten minutes on a spiritual thought, either an incident from one of the lives of the incarnations of God, the *Bhagavad Gita*, the Fourth Gospel or the *Ramayana* or a spiritual thought, and determine gently but firmly to bring the mind back from any disturbing and irrelevant lines of thought which it may raise. Do this regularly every night or morning for three weeks, keeping to the same time, and you will see for yourself how the number of distracting thoughts and interruptions will decrease and lose their force and the mind itself will begin to change its character and respect your instructions to it, not only at the time of the practice but in the rest of your life also. This is only a first step in the 'Kindergarten' of Yoga but it is a very great step indeed to recognise that we have an instrument which we can train and purify.

Some people may say, well, if that's all Yoga teaches I don't see that it's any different from autosuggestion or Pelmanism or whatever it may be. This is not all that Yoga teaches but only the beginning of it, but most of what it teaches can only be followed through practical experience.

Our teacher used to tell the story of the man who was given a little twig and told: 'If you plant this in your garden and look after it you will have roses of your own.' The man had seen the roses of his friend but he was a fool and he said: 'What nonsense! This is not a bit like them. It hasn't even got any leaves, let alone any flowers or buds. It's much too small anyway to bear flowers. I am just being led up the garden path.' And he threw the twig away. But another man, given the same gift, who planted the twig in the best soil he could find in his garden, tended it and watered it and patiently nurtured it, saw it in good time grow into a tall rosebush, blossoming with many roses of beautiful colour and form, emitting fragrance all round and visited by honey-seeking bees and the lovers of beauty.

The techniques of the Yogis may seem to us hardly more interesting than that dried twig, but their fruits will only be known by the one who absorbs them into his own being and through long and patient practice brings them to fruition.

6

Opinion and Certainty*

WHEN THE GREAT scientist Isaac Newton – perhaps the greatest scientist who has ever lived – was asked how he achieved his success in solving scientific problems, he said that it was entirely due to his capacity to pay attention to a problem. His biographer, Sullivan, says that this capacity that he had for paying attention carefully to the problem, thinking the problem over continually, perhaps for many months at a time, was developed in him by long practice to an extraordinary extent. It is known, for instance, that he used to go into long meditations, in which he was in a trance-like condition in his rooms, and often at this time he forgot to eat or forgot whether he had eaten or not when he came back to everyday life.

There are many stories of Newton which illustrate this fact. There is a very good story of his going out one day into the street on his way to lunch and he took the wrong turning. He turned left instead of right as he came down from his rooms at Trinity. He went along the street but could not remember, when he found himself there, what he had been doing. So he turned back and, when he got into the college, he automatically went back to his room. He had no lunch that day. There are many such examples from the life of Newton and the reason is, of course, that his mind was entirely occupied at that time with the problems that he was

---

*A lecture given on 17th February 1967.

studying. And this, says Newton, was the great secret of his success.

The teachings of this Yoga are offered in a spirit of service, at the command of our teacher, in order that you may turn your attention to what the Yogis tell us is the most important question which faces man: how to live really well. This is a question which hardly gets any attention at all in the ordinary way from the everyday man. We pay almost no heed to it. But until we attend to it, it will never be solved. Real success in life cannot come until we have tackled and solved this question.

The fact is that our attention is always being diverted to secondary problems, problems which, relatively speaking, are much less important to our happiness and our wellbeing than this central problem. What tremendous attention people are willing to give to the latest sensational story in the newspapers, for instance. What tremendous attention people are willing to give to pop music, or to making money, or to following their favourite sport. But these, from the point of view of their own happiness, from the point of view of their own wellbeing, are distractions, are diversions from the main stream of their life. It's thus not surprising that this problem does not get solved. Let us now turn our attention, therefore, to this question of what the Yogis say about the real end of life. The thoughts which are being offered to you are those given by our teacher, Dr Shastri, and they represent the essence of Yoga and the heart of true spirituality.

'In modern civilisation,' said Dr Shastri, 'we pay attention to bodily culture and to comfort – mostly to sense enjoyment.' But these things offer the soul no abiding satisfaction. In the great classic of Yoga, the *Bhagavad Gita,* it says, 'The pleasures born of the contact of the senses with their objects are impermanent. No wise man relies on them for delight.'[31] They are like nectar to begin with but like poison afterwards. And one remembers the words of the poet Burns: 'Pleasures are like poppies spread, you seize the flower its bloom is shed.'[32] Even many modern writers, like D. H. Lawrence and others, have to recognise this quality of sense experience, this ultimately dissatisfying characteristic of reliance on the senses for joy, for satisfaction.

The conclusion, say the Yogis, is that the raw mind, with its urges and impulses towards greater indulgence in sense pleasures, cannot be a reliable guide for man. It is not a reliable guide in its natural state. 'It has to be made into a guide; it has to be transformed into a reliable guide, by studying its dynamics and by practising those exercises which create a light in it.' These are the words of Dr Shastri. It has to be made a guide. How? By studying its dynamics and by practising those exercises which create a light in it.

One great method of helping to create light in the mind and to preserve peace in the mind is the practice of meditation. There are many institutions nowadays where one can learn almost any subject under the sun, from philosophy to carpentry. The instructions given in these institutions are excellent, but we put before you something quite different. Whatever kind of life you lead, whether you are interested in philosophy or in carpentry, if you want to be successful in any branch of life, you will not be successful, say the Yogis, unless your life is balanced and progressive. Life must be creative, creative of peace and happiness, creative of ever deepening knowledge, and conducive to the wellbeing of those amongst whom we live. We each innately feel the desire to have done something

---

[31]*Bhagavad Gita* II, 14.

[32]*Tam O'Shanter* by Robert Burns

worthwhile and – when it comes to our turn to shuffle off this mortal coil, as Shakespeare says – to have left behind something worthwhile, something good, however little that may be.

For this reason, we study the mind and how to use it well. The two great principles which, the Yogis tell us, lie behind the training of the mind are, first of all, the conscious control of attention, and secondly, the practice of stilling the mind. Firstly, the conscious control of attention, the attention by which Newton said he solved his problems. This is the secret of success according to Newton – conscious control of attention – and then the practice of stilling the mind.

We can say that normally we are only half-conscious of what is happening to our minds. When he watches a TV programme, the ordinary person watches it uncritically. He simply follows a stream of pictures which are presented on the screen before him, and he accepts them and gets carried along by them. This is a very good simile of the mind; it is exactly the same in the raw uncontrolled state of the mind. We simply sit, if you like, before the screen of the mind. The mind presents a stream of pictures, and we are carried along; we accept these pictures, and we are carried along passively wherever the pictures take us.

If we begin to examine when we are watching the TV what is actually happening to us, what is going on on the screen, what this stream of pictures is really like, we find that it is constantly changing. Sometimes we see a distant view, sometimes we see a close-up, sometimes there is a detail of a scene, and sometimes the eye seems to jump from one angle to another. And then we begin to realise that it is not just one view that we are looking at, one camera, but that there are many cameras, and while all of them are operating all the time, we only see that one camera which the director has chosen we shall see. And then we realise that this stream of images, apparently spontaneous, apparently just accepted passively, is being manipulated all the time by the director to create a particular effect on his audience.

It is exactly the same with the mind. There are hundreds of sensations and memories coming up at any moment. There are many senses functioning at every moment and receiving impressions from the environment, but we only notice on the screen of the mind what we are attending to. Just as in the case of the television, that attention can be passive, as it is in the case of the audience, or it can be active, as it is in the case of the director, so in the mind too, we can speak, as we often do, of something 'catching' our attention or 'drawing' our attention. And in that sense we are passive. Our attention is caught and we are passively following the thing that catches our attention. We also know and recognise in our own minds the process of actively concentrating on something because we have decided to concentrate. If we are to live consciously, say the Yogis, we must learn to control and direct our attention at will. As Newton said, success in solving any problem – and this applies not only to the scientific problems he was concerned with but any of the problems with which we are faced – depends on our ability to pay attention to it, to pay attention to what is important.

Well, you may ask, is this all we have to do? No. This is one side, this is one principle. But there is another very important factor. We must be able not only to exert our minds in productive thought, the Yogis tell us, we must also be able to relax them, to create inner peace in them. Not to attend, but to cut out and to exclude at times when we wish to, the bombardment of distracting and disturbing impressions which shower in upon us, and by doing that, by cutting out and excluding these inflowing sensations, to create an inner stillness in the mind.

One of the great modern Yogis, Swami Rama Tirtha, says that none of us would dream of spending a day then coming home in the evening and going to bed without washing our hands and face to get rid of the dust and dirt which has collected on them. But, he says, what about the mind? Is it not equally important to wash the mind? There are many thoughts which we don't want clinging to our mind. There are many impressions that we meet in the day which, so to speak, soil the mind and only create disturbance and anxiety. We should be able to wash the mind clean of these disturbances in the evening and in the morning, just as we wash our hands and our face. All the dust of the mental world comes off on the mind, so to speak, in the commerce of everyday life, and we need to be able to wash it.

When Shri Dadaji, our teacher's teacher, had a pupil who came to ask him how to deal with the mind, he said, 'Bring a glass of water.' The pupil said, 'I have such a difficult mind, it is so full of the wrong thoughts and I can't get over these. I can't deal with them. I can't force them out of my mind.' Shri Dadaji said, 'Bring a glass of water, and I'll show you how to do it.' He came with a glass of water, and the teacher took a handful of dust and threw it into the water so that it became cloudy. He said, 'This is a picture of your mind, and what you have to do is to clear the water. Now just leave the glass, leave the glass on one side and we will talk, and in half an hour we'll come back and look.'

When the glass was left on one side, gradually, over the half hour, all the particles of dust sank to the bottom and the water was clear and unclouded again. The teacher said, 'This is all you have to do. You don't have to fight the mind.

You don't have to force the wrong thoughts out of the mind. All you have to do is to sit, quiet, exclude the disturbing conditions, and allow the mind to become still, and in this way the mind will be cleaned.'

Our teacher, Dr Shastri, said this is the principle of meditation. One has to sit quiet. Not, he said, in a rocking chair, but quietly, either in the meditation posture or in a chair. The essence is 'quiet'. And then to cast off all worries and to breathe deeply, consciously and rhythmically, breathing the word OM, which is an ancient and holy syllable in Yoga, a symbol of the highest truth. Then breathing 'OM' in and out several times, close the eyes and the ears, and take a text for meditation, thinking of it in the heart region. Our teacher gave us this text:

> 'OM. I AM YOUR MASTER, O MY MIND. IT IS IMPERATIVE THAT YOU OBEY ME. BE STILL. THY REAL HOME AND SUPPORT IS GOD WITHIN ME. OM'

The practice is just to take the text and to think of it for a few minutes in the region of the heart. In Yoga a little practice is much more convincing than any amount of theory. To try and do such a practice either in the morning or the evening for a quarter of an hour, or even for ten minutes, for twenty days, will teach you more about your mind and will convince you more strongly of the value and power of meditation in transforming the mind, than any amount of reading or listening to lectures. This, then, is one of the practices which Dr Shastri gave us on which to start in meditation, and it is a practice in the stilling and concentration of the mind.

Samuel Butler, in his *Notebooks*, says, 'We are like thistle-down blown about by the wind – up and down, here and there – but not one in a thousand ever getting beyond seed-hood.'[33] Well, it's very true, but we are wrong if we think that it is the outer circumstances that blow us this way and that. We are not so much at the mercy of the outer circumstances as at the mercy of our raw and undisciplined mind, because until we have made the mind into a reliable guide, it does blow us this way and that way. As the *Gita* says, 'The mind, driven by the roving senses, is like a ship blown hither and thither at the mercy of the rising wind.'[34] Therefore, to keep a watch over the mind and to attend to what is worthwhile, to still the mind in meditation each day in the morning, is a great means of transforming the mind and, through it, transforming our life.

Even in ordinary life we choose from an endless variety of ongoing impressions and topics. Like the television director who is surrounded by a dozen different views from his various cameras, so we too can choose from the many possibilities that life presents to us. By choosing wisely we can live creatively. Not only at the time of meditation, not only at the time when we are thinking about the spiritual practices or the teachings of Yoga, but even at other times we can keep the mind usefully employed and attending to the right things. There is a poem by the Japanese monk Basho, in which he says: 'I am like one who eats breakfast gazing on the morning glory.' The morning glory, as you know, is a very beautiful flower which blossoms only for a few days in Japan, and in this short Haiku verse, the poet expresses the thought that even in the most worldly surroundings, even when one is eating breakfast, even in the most pedestrian occupation, we can keep our minds filled with the best thoughts.

---

[33]*The Note-Books of Samuel Butler*, Ch1, 1917.

[34]*Bhagavad Gita* II, 67.

Dr Shastri used to say that life should progress on all planes, not only material but also ethical, aesthetic and spiritual. 'Scoop up the water and the moon is in your hands; hold the flowers and your clothes are scented with them.' The meaning is that we must make efforts, for it is by our own striving that we can achieve and increase our own light. Not just to admire the spiritual teachings, but actually to make efforts to follow them. 'Scoop up the water' means to collect the mind, to protect it from the outer circumstances and to still the ruffled surface of the water. By scooping up the water we have it in our hands and, protecting this pool of water, we can see the moon in it. So by controlling the mind, by withdrawing the mind at the time of meditation, the innate light of the spirit, which is the moon, will shine reflected in the mind and we will have inner peace and illumination.

However, Dr Shastri warned: 'One of the greatest impediments to spiritual progress, is the strongly entrenched sense of individuality.' Every man is in a certain sense a multitude while in the absolute sense he is a spiritual unity.

Isaac Newton was not only a great scientific genius, as we said, perhaps the greatest of all time, but he was also a very spiritual man with a profound interest in mysticism, particularly the mysticism of Jakob Böhme. At the time he lived, in the seventeenth century, there were a number of people in England who were devoted to the foundation of modern science and who formed between them the Royal Society which still exists today and is, of course, a very eminent body of scientists. In those days it was really a handful of amateurs who were enthusiasts for science – which was then in its infancy – men like Robert Boyle, Halley (who gave his name to the comet which he discovered), Sir Christopher Wren who, as well as being an architect, was a great scientist, and many others. Among those others was Robert Hooke who was, himself, a very able scientist. He was the man who discovered the laws of elasticity: Hooke's Law. Robert Hooke could have been very content to make his contribution to science, if he hadn't been a man who was eaten up by a sense of exaggerated individuality. He was a most conceited man and he was inordinately jealous of Isaac Newton, whom he consciously or unconsciously recognised to be better than he was. He couldn't bear to think that anyone was a greater man than Robert Hooke. This sense of individuality clouded his judgement and it eventually led him into frank deceit and dishonesty.

The contrast between Newton and Hooke is very revealing, and it has spiritual relevance to the teachings of Yoga and what we are dealing with here. We find that Newton in his discoveries never wanted to claim a monopoly for his inventions. He was quite indifferent, in fact, to name and fame. He had to be persuaded almost always by his friends to publish those of his results which he did publish, and there were many which he didn't. He disliked very much the argumentation and the criticism which went on after publication, by people who hadn't thought about things properly and who hadn't done the experiments but who nonetheless thought that they were qualified to get up and make criticisms. He disliked these most of all, he said, because they disturbed his meditations and prevented him from getting on with his discoveries. He once wrote: 'What's done before many witnesses [he means in a public meeting] is seldom without some further concern than that for truth.' They are very true words. Throughout his life in his scientific work he had the idea of a quiet quest for the truth. As a consequence, he kept many of his greatest discoveries to himself for a number of years, and he never denied anyone else the claim to have independently discovered the same things that he had discovered. In fact, the only thing which roused him to defend himself in public was the charge that he had stolen his ideas from other people.

Now Hooke was quite a different sort of person. He, on the contrary, was always making big claims which he couldn't make good and, needless to say, charged Newton, who had really discovered them before, with pinching the ideas from him. Newton, we now know, discovered the Law of Gravitation – the great law that bodies are attracted to each other in proportion to the inverse square of their distance apart – in his twenty-fifth year when he was up in Lincolnshire because of plague in Cambridge. But he kept it to himself and published nothing about his discovery of gravitation until twenty years later when he produced the *Principia.*

Hooke, on the other hand, had a very vague idea about gravitation eighteen years later, and so did a number of other people like Wren and Halley, but none of them were able to solve the mathematical problems concerned with it, which Newton had solved long before. Hooke, who didn't want to admit it, told his friends that he had done it all, but because other people wouldn't value it if he published it straight away, he was going to keep it to himself, and he would tell them in due course. But of course, he never did so because he hadn't done it.

Eventually, Newton was prevailed on to publish the Law of Gravitation in the *Principia* and he included the results that he had found so many years before. As soon as the manuscript was sent to the press, Hooke began claiming that his name should be entered in the manuscript as being the true discoverer of Gravitation. An example of Newton's attitude to this was that, though he didn't believe Hooke's claim, he suggested in the end: 'By all means let's settle this and we'll put a little clause in the thing to say this was independently discovered by Hooke.' This wasn't in fact the case, but Hooke was so jealous and vain that he wrote a long and totally false account, an account which he knew to be untrue, and got another person, John Aubrey, to write to somebody who was publishing a history of Oxford, giving a long account of how Hooke had discovered it and Newton had pinched the idea from him. This is all on record.

Now, the contrast between the behaviour of Newton and Hooke is a perfect example of the contrast between wisdom and spiritual ignorance. Hooke wasn't ignorant intellectually – he was a very clever and able man – but he was an ignoramus compared with Isaac Newton in the spiritual sense. His great gifts, and all that he had genuinely contributed to science, didn't prevent him, because of his inordinate vanity and conceit and his longing to copyright to himself what didn't really belong to him, from stooping to become a liar and a cheat.

We can say that this is a picture from history of the unspiritualised mind. When Dr Shastri says, 'The greatest impediment spiritually is the strongly entrenched sense of individuality,' Hooke provides a very good example of this. Unless this narrow sense of individuality, of wanting to appropriate to oneself every advantage, even at the expense of truth and righteousness, is eradicated, the truth will not stay with us. This is the main problem – the problem of the exaggerated ego of man. It is the main obstacle in spiritual life, and it is not dealt with by intellectual learning, nor by skill, nor by cleverness. It is only dealt with through the spiritual training and the cultivation of universal love and wisdom.

We have to forget individuality, say the Yogis, through sacrifice, service, devotion, meditation and love of truth. This attitude of separateness is as unnatural as a boil, and this is shown, they say, by the fact that it is not present when the mind is really focussed with deep interest on any worthwhile object. If we are listening with real attention to, say, Beethoven's Ninth Symphony or a great speech of Shakespeare, then there is an absence in the mind of this sense of individuality and there is an experience of joy. Swami Rama Tirtha speaks of it as 'the little copyrighting self' and he says that it is the main cause of spiritual opacity in the mind.

'What is it that dampens your spirits and your cheerfulness?' he asks. 'It is what is called spiritual opacity. You have to make your mind transparent. You have to give up the opacity in you. It darkens you. What is this opacity? It is this little ego – this proprietary self which says, "This is mine; this belongs to me"'.

We have to dissolve this dark and opaque screen of egoity or it will lead us astray and blind our vision. How, then, are we to do this? What is the method that the Yogis give? It is by forgetting it, by not attending to it continually as we do in ordinary life but, like Newton, turning our minds to science, to art, to literature, to truth, to beauty, and to the spiritual teachings. 'Your opacity is gone,' says Rama Tirtha, 'When you have in mind no rivalry, no claims for yourself, when you apply this test to your soul and see that all those of whom you used to be jealous are felt as being fellow beings and as part of the same unity.'

At present we are fragments, say the Yogis, because we are conscious of the difference between man and man, between thing and thing. 'It is only when we can feel unity in all, that peace, benediction and congratulation will issue, not only from our own mind, but from every blade of grass and from every twinkling star.' It is not an exaggeration, says Dr Shastri, but a fact experienced by so many saints, that can be experienced by you too, through experiment. To experience the truth is to be whole – to lift up the mind from the region of differences, and to let it dwell in unity and identity. The methods of attaining it should be natural, because the attainment is natural, and not by means of starving or torturing the body; not by the now popular, but very mistaken, psychedelic drugs as they are called, but by natural means – natural means because the state is natural. This opacity in the mind is unnatural, say the Yogis.

Water can be either cooled and frozen, or heated and boiled, and we can see what a great difference there is between ice and boiling water in their properties. It is the same with the mind. It has two states like this. But there is also a third way – to vaporise the water, and so with the mind. We can see that lethargy and love of comfort freeze the mind, so to speak, rendering it indifferent to anybody or to anything else. On the other hand, passions cause the mind to boil and it loses the faculty of right judgement. But there is a third way – to lighten the mind and focus it on truth through meditation. We should neither let it freeze nor boil – we should focus it through meditation.

I end with another verse from the Far East:[35] 'Our body is the bodhi tree and our mind a mirror bright. Carefully we wipe them hour by hour and let no dust alight.' The dust that alights on the mind, is the dust of the world and the desire to mount on the heads of others. This is the sense of exaggerated individuality or egoity, overburdened with aggression and conceit. The mind has to be wiped hour by hour so that this dust does not alight on it and in this way it becomes a mirror in which the highest light in the being of man shines. A man discovers that within the essence of his

---

[35]Written by Shen-hsui (AD 605–706) when he was a student.

own personality is a divine principle – Truth or God – that principle from which the world springs up, in which it exists and in which it is finally dissolved – a principle of infinite awareness and infinite consciousness. This illumination is the goal of Yoga.

7

Knowledge in Action*

IN *The Doctor's Dilemma*, George Bernard Shaw enjoys himself at the expense of the medical profession and he makes many shrewd and telling criticisms, some perhaps more apposite when he was writing than they are today, because after all this play was written in 1906, but many of them are still very relevant. He collects a group of doctors on the stage and he makes it perfectly clear that the diagnosis any particular patient is going to get, depends not on what is wrong with him but on which of the doctors he goes to.

To the eminent surgeon, Cutler Walpole in the play, all the patients who come to him are suffering from chronic blood poisoning due to the decaying food matter in the nuciform sac, and the solution, of course, is to have him remove the nuciform sac. Shaw makes someone ask him whether he himself has had his sac removed, and he replies that he is one of the lucky five per cent of the population who has not got a nuciform sac! The other character, Sir Ralph Bloomfield Bonington, believes that the main cause of illness is infection with a pathogen and once one has sought out and destroyed the pathogen all will be well – a very orthodox view, no doubt.

Sir Colenso Ridgeon was really a very thinly disguised portrait of a real doctor, Sir Almroth Wright, who was Shaw's friend and, as you may know, the teacher of

*A lecture given on 17th March 1967.

Sir Alexander Fleming, the discoverer of penicillin (there is still a Wright Institute in St Mary's Hospital). To him all his patients are suffering from allergy or, as he puts it in the play, a deficiency of obsolin, the substance with which germs must be buttered in order to make phagocytes eat them up.

One of the last doctors that Shaw introduces, Blenkinsop, is a humble GP in the East End of London. He has one great panacea which he gives to all his patients for all their ills: a pound of ripe greengages every day half an hour before lunch.

Now, the point that Shaw makes is that each of them is to some extent a successful doctor. But we can surely see that a science of medicine in which the diagnosis of human illness tells us more about the doctor who is making the diagnosis than about the patient is in a fairly primitive state. It is indeed hardly beyond its infancy. Well, I think we can say confidently nowadays that, with regard to physical illness at least, we have got beyond this stage in medicine. With regard to mental illness it is much less clear, especially if methods of treatment are considered. But with regard to man's spiritual problems, we are surely still in very much the position which Shaw depicted. This applies alike to the diagnosis of the human situation and the cure which is prescribed for that illness. This being so, all that is left to us is to choose our doctor wisely.

Man is, after all, presented with a whole series of claims by those who promise him lasting satisfaction and a degree of freedom if he will follow their particular panacea. He is promised political panaceas, social panaceas, aesthetic panaceas or religious panaceas. Some people tell him he must take psychedelic drugs. Other people tell him the only solution is in world Communism or in Humanism or in

Christian Science. Well, at any rate one can say there is at least agreement among all people who offer these panaceas that there is a real problem for man, a real problem of which he is perhaps only dimly aware, which requires a solution.

Another feature of the views put forward by Shaw's doctors, we can say, is that they are all eminently reasonable. Given their point of view, each one can put up a really argued and indeed convincing view for their particular approach. As Alexander Pope ironically says: 'When doctors disagree who shall decide?' And the conclusion we must come to is that mere logic and mere cleverness are not enough to solve men's problems. We need something more than this. One might say we could learn from that much more modern invention, the computer, in this matter. Computers, as you know, are machines for carrying out logical reasoning *par excellence*. And we find, if we go to the computer experts, that computers make mistakes and arrive at the wrong conclusions, just as human logicians do. But they do this most often, not because they make logical errors or because their reasoning apparatus goes wrong, but because they are working on false premises. It is the original program of instructions to the computer which is found to be incorrect. Something vital has been overlooked in giving the computer its instructions as to what to do and the result is that it is wrong.

Logically speaking, computers work very fast indeed, far faster than any human brain can work. What in fact takes time in using computers and often wastes energy and money at enormous length and in huge quantities is working out the correct program of instructions. When one puts an instruction in and gets the wrong answers, one has to find out what is wrong with the program, and it is again the experience of those who use these machines that this finding out of what is wrong is often a very difficult process, even in quite simple computations.

Well, it is exactly the same with solving the human problem. Our minds may be very quick and very brilliant, say the Yogis, though obviously not as quick in logical thinking as a computer. What takes time and what makes our mental energy often go largely to waste is faulty programming, that is to say, the fact that we work on the wrong instructions, that we argue from false premises. We can say that life poses us all with a problem and we have to find out how to solve it. Usually it is not reason which leads us astray, it is the premises on which we are working.

So the starting point for one of the great insights in the Yoga doctrine is that we should put aside once and for all the modern heresy that we can solve all our problems by mere cleverness. Perhaps twentieth century man relies far too much on his intellect – it is a very faulty instrument. It very easily reasons but it easily reasons on the basis of false programs, programs such as the love of pleasure or self-aggrandisement or ambition. These lead man to the wrong conclusion and they don't end by giving him the peace and satisfaction which he wants. How rationally, one might say, Adolf Hitler argued his case for the elimination of the Jews, or Stalin planned the liquidation of his comrades of the Russian Revolution, in the late 1920s and 1930s. The intellect of Friedrich Nietzsche landed him finally only in the madhouse.

What then, according to the teaching of this Yoga, is the something more that we need? What is this something else that we need? It is wisdom, not cleverness but wisdom. We need to be wise and to know the real goal of our life. We need to know, to ask, what is the greatest good that we are capable of aiming for, and how can we aspire to that greatest good? In the computer, the goal or aim of the logic, of the logical computation, does not depend on the machine, it depends entirely on the programmer. But man is in a different situation. He is a living organism. He himself, in the modern jargon, is a goal seeking device. What is the real goal of man's endeavours? What is it that his heart and his soul really desire and want and what will satisfy the inner urges that he has? This is the great question that faces us in life.

It is that goal, say the Yogis, on attaining which he will satisfy all the desires of his heart, and will enjoy the freedom and happiness for which his soul craves. Will his soul be satisfied by the pursuit of the will-o'-the-wisp of sense pleasures or ambition? No, say the Yogis. There is a verse by the Japanese poet Isha who lived in the eighteenth century: 'Little knowing that the tree will soon be cut down, the birds are building their nests upon it.' The meaning is: man relies, until he becomes wise, on the passing objects outside to give him satisfaction, but he is building on shifting sand. He is building his nest in the tree which is going to be cut down tomorrow, and in this way he is not going to achieve what he wants to achieve.

What then is the wisdom that we need to cultivate? We can say that it concerns our feelings as much as our thoughts, our desires as much as our arguments, our aims as much as our reasoning. We are very keen in the West, in this advanced civilisation, on educating our minds, but we neglect to educate our feelings. We need, say the Yogis, to refine our feelings and to channel them towards what will be creative of our good and our happiness in the long run. Ultimately our good and our happiness are not separable from the wellbeing and happiness of the society in which we live.

One of the great contemporary philosophers of the West, Bertrand Russell, makes a point which is very close to the yogic teaching, when he says that we should ask what wisdom is and then set out to teach it. He says that clearly, though we all agree that our own age surpasses all previous ages in knowledge, what it lacks is wisdom, and he then goes on to consider what wisdom is. He analyses it provisionally into certain elements. First of all, he says, wisdom implies a sense of proportion, and secondly it implies a comprehensive vision, taking everything into account, and an awareness of the ends of human life, not just acting on the moment, but an awareness of the ends of human life. He says that the comprehensive vision should include not only the intellect but also the feelings. 'It is by no means uncommon,' says Russell, 'to find men whose knowledge is wide but whose feelings are narrow. Such men lack what I am calling wisdom.'

Here is another passage:

> 'We study the composition of an atom from a disinterested desire for knowledge [and he is here stressing the danger of knowledge without wisdom] and incidentally place in the hands of powerful lunatics the means of destroying the human race. In such ways the pursuit of knowledge may become harmful unless it is combined with wisdom. And wisdom in the sense of comprehensive vision is not necessarily present in specialists in the pursuit of knowledge. The essence of wisdom is emancipation as far as possible from the tyranny of the here and now. We cannot help the egoism of our senses; sight and sound and touch are bound up with our own bodies and cannot be made impersonal.'[36]

---

[36]Bertrand Russell, 'Knowledge and wisdom', in *Portraits from Memory and Other Essays*, 1954.

But he goes on to say that, as the infant grows and his horizons widen, so he becomes less bound up with the mere egoity, the mere individual outlook of his own body and his own physical personality. And in this sense, says Russell, he achieves growing wisdom. 'It is this approach towards impartiality that constitutes growth and wisdom. Can wisdom in this sense be taught, and if it can, should the teaching of it be one of the main aims of education? I should answer both these questions in the affirmative.'[37]

This is what an eminent Western thinker thinks. And it is the objective of the Yoga which we are teaching to liberate man from the narrowness of individualistic feelings and from the narrowness of the unenlightened, the unrefined, mind. Our feelings and our values, no less than our intellect, are all-important in life. It is the rightness of these as much as the keenness of our mind which constitutes being wise. A computer may be a better logician than a man, but it can never be wise as a man can be wise, for this concerns his values and his desires. It concerns, in a word, what he really loves. It was the teaching of Sigmund Freud that life force and love force are basically one and the same. And we can say that the quality of life is the quality of what a man really loves. To know what is really valuable and to love, that is one of the great secrets of success in life.

In one of his poems, Walt Whitman describes attending a lecture on astronomy. The poem is as follows:[38]

> When I heard the learn'd astronomer;
> When the proofs of figures were ranged in columns before me,

---

[37]Bertrand Russell, 'Knowledge and wisdom', in *Portraits from Memory and Other Essays*, 1954.
[38]Walt Whitman, 'When I Heard the Learn'd Astronomer'.

When I was shown the charts and diagrams,
To add, divide and measure them,
When I, sitting, heard the astronomer,
Where he lectured, with much applause in the lecture-room,
How soon, unaccountable, I became tired and sick,
Till arising and gliding out I wander'd off by myself,
In the mystical moist night air, and from time to time,
Look'd up in perfect silence at the stars.

Why was Whitman sickened? What is it that Whitman is expressing here? He was sickened because he implies the astronomers only expressed, for all their learning and their knowledge, their own self-love and their own conceit, not the love of the beauty of the stars. They were still theoreticians – it was still talk about the stars which he got from them and not experience of the stars, not a direct view of the beauty of the night sky. They had not escaped from the tyranny of the individual ego.

The conclusion is that we need not only intellectual enquiry, not only theoretical knowledge of Yoga, or indeed of any other subject, but also actually to educate the mind and the emotions, to refine and channel the inner urges towards the higher ideal. In other words, we need the right faith. Theoretical knowledge never truly becomes a man's until he can transform it into a practical faith. Now faith is a word that we don't like nowadays, which tends to make people shy off, but it doesn't mean in this sense a blind belief. It means directing the emotions and the will to execute a plan which has been already well scrutinised and adopted by reason and intuition. This is the meaning of faith in the yogic teachings, in the yogic sense. And unless we engage the whole of our being, unless in Russell's sense we engage our feelings not merely our mind, we shall never make any knowledge we have creative. It is only when the thing engages our feelings and our being that we begin to bring our knowledge into action.

So not blind faith, say the Yogis, we need a wise faith. The *Bhagavad Gita*, the great classic of Yoga, speaks in the seventeenth chapter of faith.

> 'The faith of each is in accordance with his nature… The man is made up of his faith; as a man's faith is, so is he.' (Chapter XVII, verse 3)

The meaning here is that faith is not something that you have or don't have; it is something in fact that everyone has. What is different is the quality of this element in the personality, this deep-seated element in different people. It may be a faith in materialism; it may be a faith in the fundamental badness of the world; it may be a faith which is a spiritual faith. Whatever it is, there is in each and every person, say the Yogis, this deep-seated element in our being, engaging our emotions, the driving force behind our life, and it is this faith which has to be wise if we are to live successfully, because it is the spring of action and the spring of creativity within the personality. Until we have a faith, so to speak, we do not transform our emotions and until we engage our emotions we shall not be creative. Our teacher used to say: 'Without faith there can be no devotion.' Theoretical knowledge is possible without faith but wisdom is only possible through the cultivation of faith.

Let us consider a little further, then, what we mean by faith. It has something to do with belief. But what then is belief, psychologically speaking? If you ask Western psychologists like James or Russell, they will say that belief is an idea in the mind combined with what one might call a 'yes feeling'. We have an idea in the mind, we feel, yes, this is so. Disbelief, of course, is an idea combined with a no feeling, but we can ignore this complication for the present discussion. So an idea combined with a 'yes feeling' is the psychological explanation of belief. But there is, of course, more than one kind of 'yes feeling', and more than one degree of conviction in belief. We can very easily agree with something mildly, without it making the slightest difference to us in life or indeed in thought. We can even assent to something intellectually without really agreeing to it.

There is a very good example given by the American psychologist, Erich Fromm, when he describes a questionnaire which was sent out in the Deep South in America, the first question of which was: 'Are all men equal?' And to this question eighty-five per cent of the populace answered yes. Another question was: 'Are Negros equal to whites?' And the answers for that were twenty per cent yes. So quite clearly there was something which was intellectually assented to, the idea that all men are equal, but in fact this wasn't really so, the people didn't really agree with this.

John Henry Newman, in his *Grammar of Assent*, written in the nineteenth century, says that there are two kinds of assent or 'yes feeling': what he called 'notional assent' and what he called 'real assent'. He said you can agree with an abstract idea or notion in principle, and this is simply notional assent; we may think that we agree with it. It doesn't really make any difference. It is simply notional assent. It is quite different from the kind of assent that we have when we say that we believe in our friends or in our house or in this table or in the existence of the other people in the room. This is a real assent. We really believe this, we have a deep conviction. And he said that the real characteristic of these two types of assent is that in notional assent we are usually agreeing to something, just an idea, just an abstract principle and it is not real and direct and immediate to us, but in real assent the thing that we really believe in is something that we know directly, which we see like the table and the door and the room. Only with real assent, not with notional assent, do we get deep conviction. A viewpoint, it was said recently, a viewpoint, a theory, only becomes a standpoint when we can put our weight on it. It is a very good epigram, I think: 'A viewpoint only becomes a standpoint when we can put our weight on it.' Notional assent, assent just in theory, is no use in practice, because we can't put our weight on it, we can't rely on it. When the test comes in action, then we shall find out that we don't really believe it. Only when it becomes a real assent can it be tested in action.

Faith in the sense in which the *Bhagavad Gita* speaks of it is a real assent to something. It is the kind of feeling within the personality which alters our life and our action. Not the agreement of a politician – and they are, after all, always reaching agreements – because the agreement of a politician is only notional assent. Usually, at least, what they really believe is different from what they say, and it reveals itself sooner or later in their action. What we need is real assent, real belief, because it is this which changes our life, within our personality.

If man asks what the great influences in history have been, if one thinks of any of the great figures in history, for instance, St Joan or, if you like, Lenin or any others – who were the people who really made an impact on history and changed the course of the world? They were people who had a real faith. People who had a real belief in something, and this in itself has been creative and transformative.

What we need, then, is the right faith, and this, if we are to believe Newman, can only be firmly based on the possibility of something immediately experienced. If man is to have a firm basis for his spiritual faith, he must have the possibility of immediately experiencing something within his being which establishes its spiritual nature. It mustn't be blind faith or notional assent, but he needs wisdom based on the realisation of the spiritual element in his own being. And this indeed is the aim of Yoga.

Is there such an element in the human personality? Newman held that God is present and manifest in every man as the light of conscience in the mind. From the yogic point of view it is a provisional truth and really only a half-truth. Yoga holds that there is within each man a spiritual element, his own real Self. 'O Arjuna,' says the Lord in the *Gita*, 'I abide deep in the hearts of all beings.'[39] The Yoga doctrine is the same as the doctrine of the Quakers in the West who speak of the Inner Light, the seed of God in all men. The Yogis say that when man awakens to a conscious realisation of this element, his real Self, then he is no longer dependent on the notional assent to a theoretical or an abstract idea. His faith, if you like, is based on the real assent in something known to him directly in his own experience. 'When a man becomes as firmly convinced of his identity with God,' says Shri Shankara, 'as he is now in his identity with the body, then he becomes consciously immortal.' Then he is an enlightened Yogi, says Shri Shankara. Then he passes beyond the realm of opinion to the realm of certainty.

This wisdom, or real knowledge, which is the aim of Yoga, is only to be achieved by active experiment and enquiry, not simply by theoretical speculation. We have, say the Yogis, to transform the mind into a source of light and peace and goodwill by conscious effort. We can learn only by trying in practice. Hidden treasure, says Shri Shankara,

---

[39]*Bhagavad Gita* X, 20; XIII, 17; XV, 15 and XVIII, 61.

will not come forth unless we dig. We have to dig for this treasure – it's no good just simply saying, come forth! We have to make active efforts. Man's spiritual malady will not be cured, even if we reach the right diagnosis, without carrying out the necessary treatment, not merely by knowing the necessary treatment.

One of the great Sufi mystics, Al-Ghazali, who was at the time one of the most learned, most successful and most eminent teachers of his day in the University of Baghdad, suddenly realised that knowing, as he did, all the classics of the Sufis and knowing all about the Sufi mystic path was not the same as practising it or travelling that path. He was a very sincere man and he decided that he had been wrong in just relying on the theoretical knowledge. He gave up all his riches and his position at that time, because he wanted to follow this path. He became a spiritual pupil again and realised in practice what he had only known in theory. This is the way to recognise the importance of the practical knowledge.

One of the great modern Yogis, Swami Rama Tirtha, says that though the intellect may establish the validity of a doctrine in theory, the realisation only comes through its becoming a living faith. He says: 'The ego is the seal on the treasury which is hidden within thee; why not break the seal and enjoy the wealth of the universe?' We have, through the practice of meditation, through the practice of this Yoga, to dissolve the individuality in service, devotion and knowledge – to dismount, so to speak, from the individuality.

I end with another verse by the eighteenth century Japanese poet Isha: 'Lo! the cherry-blossoms have forced a *daimio* to dismount.' Even the self-assertive noble warrior dismounts when he sees the beauty of the cherries in blossom, says the poet. In the spiritual meaning, the combative, self-assertive ego of the human mind in its raw state, has to dismount from the personality before the beauty and majesty of the spiritual truth. Then, say the Yogis, when this is done, through the practice of Yoga, man is born again in his own true nature as a spiritual being and regains his birthright. Let us each day begin to learn to forget the ego in meditation on the highest truth, on the spiritual truth. If we do so, say the Yogis, the personality will gradually be transformed and we shall become a source of peace and light to ourselves and to others.

8

Beyond Action*

MYSTICISM IN THE West has always tended to be indentified with quietism. And quietism, as the Oxford Dictionary defines it, means a passive attitude towards life, with devotional contemplation and abandonment of the will. And the dictionary goes on to give the secondary meaning of non-resistant principles. Therefore, mysticism for most Westerners implies non-resistance and passive inaction. And this is why the *Bhagavad Gita* comes as such a salutary corrective to the average Westerner. Here, after all, is one of the world's great classics of mysticism, which begins with the hero, Prince Arjuna, advocating everything which we might imagine was admirable and in tune with the true mystic tradition. Faced with the prospect of fighting in a war, and the almost inevitable consequence that he will be involved in the killing of his opponents, among whom are a number of people whom he knows and admires – relatives and friends – he firmly decides that the right course is for him to become a quietist, and to adopt the path of non-resistance and pacifism.

As the first chapter of the *Gita* tells us:

> 'There saw Arjuna standing, fathers and grandfathers, teachers, uncles, brothers, sons, and grandsons and also companions. When the son of Kunti saw

*A lecture given on 11th October 1974.

all those kinsmen thus standing arrayed, he was overcome with great compassion, and uttered these words in sadness:

"When I see my own people arrayed and eager for fight, O Krishna, my limbs quail, my mouth goes dry, my body shakes, my hair stands on end. The bow slips from my hand and my skin too is burning all over. I am not able to stand steadily; my mind is reeling. I see evil omens, nor do I foresee any good by slaying my own people in the fight. I do not long for victory, O Krishna, nor kingdom, nor pleasures. Of what use is the kingdom to us, or enjoyment or even life? Those for whose sake we desire kingdoms, enjoyments and pleasures, they stand here in battle renouncing their lives and riches. These I would not consent to kill, even though killed myself. Even for the kingdom of the three worlds, how much less for the sake of the earth. What pleasures can be ours, O Krishna, after we have slain the sons of Dhritarashtra? Only sin will accrue to us if we kill them. It is not right that we slay our kinsmen. Indeed how can we be happy if we kill our own people? Even if those whose minds are over-powered by greed see no wrong in the destruction of the family, and no crime and treachery to friends, why should we not have the wisdom to turn them away from this sin, O Krishna? We who see the wrong in the destruction of the family.'"[40]

Arjuna goes on to expound the general social consequences, which we know so well, of war and the breakdown of social

---

[40]*Bhagavad Gita* I, 21 et seq.

life. 'In the ruin of a family,' he says, 'its ancient laws are destroyed, and when the laws perish the whole family yields to lawlessness.' How *many* times in the modern world have we experienced, (at least second hand if not directly) the dire consequences of the breakdown of law and order, in the wake of civil strife? 'Alas, what a great sin we have resolved to commit,' Arjuna says, 'striving to slay our own people, through our own greed for pleasures of the kingdom. Far better would it be for me that the sons of Dhritarashtra, with weapons in hand, should slay me in the battle, while I remain unresisting and unarmed.'

Well, I think that many people who read the *Gita* forget to read the first chapter. Perhaps they read it on the first occasion that they read the book, and then they turn and say: 'No, the main part of the *Gita* is chapters two to eighteen.' But it is good to remind ourselves of this first chapter, because it is an eloquent appeal to the doctrine of quietism, and we might well expect when we first come upon this great speech of Arjuna's that the rest of the work would consist of a eulogy of the noble stand that Arjuna has made, an account of how his nobility in adopting the path of pacifism has led to a reconciliation between the warring factions, or at least to a new impetus to others to follow his inspiring example. Well, as we know, not a bit of it. The rest of this great spiritual classic is an uninhibited exposure of the wrong-headedness of Arjuna's stand, not on the grounds that it is too spiritual and other-worldly, but on the precisely opposite grounds that it is not spiritual enough. It is based only on looking at the surface of things and not below the surface.

This refutation in the rest of the *Gita*, starts by turning a searching and penetrating eye on the whole nature of action. What is action and what do we do it for? Now the curious thing about action is that one can look at it in two completely different fashions, and both are equally valid in their own way.

One can ask of an action: 'What causes it?' but equally, one can ask of it: 'For what purpose is it done?' These two simple questions hide diametrically opposed points of view, so diametrically opposed in fact, that they are literally facing in opposite directions, because the first question looks backwards and the second question looks forwards. The first – 'What causes it?' – leads to causal explanations. It seeks the earlier events which led inevitably to the present action, and its explanations provide chains of successive causes and events leading ever backwards into the unknown past. These chains have no end unless, like Aristotle, one invokes that mysterious First Cause, or Prime Mover, which is supposed to have started the whole process of causality in the first place.

The second way of looking at action, asking the question: 'For what purpose is it done?' looks forward, and it leads to teleological explanations. There is a network of purposes leading forward to subsidiary or major ends, or goals, and again losing themselves in the mists of an unknown future unless, like St Thomas Aquinas and others, we invoke the notion of a final goal and aim, or *summum bonum*, to which all action is ultimately leading us.

But if we give up trying either to trace action backwards causally to the distant past, or to trace it forwards into the mists of the future by seeking the purpose of it all, we can narrow down our gaze and look instead at action here and now, and try to find out what its present nature is. We can ask: 'Why do we do what we do, here and now? What guides and governs our own action in daily life, and is it effectively bringing about the results which we desire?'

The desired result – yes, certainly that is one clue to the nature of action. Clearly, in our own life the desired result is one of the most important determinants of much of our action.

One of the greatest urges to action, after all, seems to be wish-fulfilment, the urge to realise some particular desire which we have harboured. And there is no shortage of advice for those who want to act in this way. Indeed, the individual is surrounded by advisers, good, indifferent and bad, advisers who are continually saying to him in effect: 'If you want something we can tell you how to get it' – financial advisers, business advisers, advisers in matters of the heart, even advisers about where to go on holiday, what to wear, how to speak, how to win friends and influence people. It can be said of all these advisers that they tell you the appropriate course of action which you should take in order to achieve the desired end, and this course of action, incidentally, very often includes, and it is of course purely incidental, doing something which brings the adviser himself a substantial reward. Moreover, such advice is not limited to the secular part of our lives. The *Gita* makes clear that it applies no less to the religious part as well. One of the most surprising things about the *Gita*, even in the second chapter at the beginning of the exposition, is its sweeping dismissal of the bulk of the traditional religious literature as being no more than a glorified version of advice of this sort.

It is, according to the *Gita*, and I am quoting verses forty-two and forty-three of chapter two: 'The undiscerning, whose nature is desire, they are the kind of people who are intent on heaven, who rejoice in the letter of the Veda and contend that there is nothing else.' These undiscerning ones are always seeking some Eldorado, some Shangri-La which will fulfil their desires. That Heaven may be thought of, then, either as here, or as there, it makes no difference. It may be a heaven on earth, or it may be a heaven after death, but it is a dream place, a lotus land – the land where the rainbow ends. Such undiscerning ones lay down various specialised courses of action for the attainment of enjoyment and power. And they proclaim with great eloquence, or to put it literally in the words of the *Gita* 'with flowery words', the delightful fruits which accrue from such actions.

This, then, is one of the attitudes towards action: that it is the means to wish-fulfilment, just that, no more and no less. And I think a moment's thought should remind us that this is a peculiarly modern attitude. We act, says modern man, to gratify our desires. And if you do not think that this is immediately convincing, perhaps you might like to see a secular manifestation of this point of view. All you need do is to buy the colour supplements of any of the Sunday newspapers, which each week regale us with sleek and colourful advertisements of desirable things: cars, television sets, stereo and quadraphonic record players, bigger and better gadgets, guaranteed by the advertisements to transform our life here into heaven on earth. It is in fact the philosophy of the consumer society. But as Professor Galbraith has wisely pointed out, in modern industrial society it is not just a question of supplying an existing demand. It is, much more subtly and sinisterly, a question of actually creating it. People must be made to crave what it is that the manufacturers have to offer. This is logically unavoidable.

To develop a new car, or a new sophisticated washing machine, is an extremely expensive project taking much capital and many years. Companies have to plan very far ahead. When the essential decisions to go ahead with such new products are made, the products themselves will still not be available to the public for many years. And since the consciousness that they will eventually exist has not even begun to penetrate into the most forward-looking of the potential consumers, there is, therefore, no question of the product being made to satisfy an already felt demand. On the contrary, the development of the product must go hand-in-hand with the creation of the demand for it. And so the whole sophisticated apparatus of market research and advertising, followed up by sales promotion goes into operation. The whole system becomes its own *raison d'être*. People work to supply what they imagine to be their own needs, but their efforts to create wealth for themselves are expended in the end on luxuries that they have been persuaded are essentials to their wellbeing.

Now this would not be so bad if the promised heaven on earth materialised, but the demands are never met, because the promised satisfaction does not come. And so feeling still dissatisfied but assured by the advertisers and the hidden persuaders that Elysium is only just round the corner, they are persuaded that all they need is yet more wealth to spend on yet greater luxuries – and so it goes on. With this philosophy the standard of living may indeed rise, but surely the quality of life goes down. No wonder that the *Gita* says that it is the undiscerning who follow this philosophy of action, as the means to the attainment of enjoyment and power. 'Those whose minds are carried away by this doctrine,' it says, 'are not concentrated and are not established in the Self.'[41]

Clearly then, the view that action is simply for wish-fulfilment will not do. And man, if he is wise, must stand back and take a closer look at action. Like Arjuna, he must ask himself: 'What am I doing all this for? Is this really what

---

[41] *Bhagavad Gita* II, 44.

I want?' Arjuna may not have been right, but at least he had the beginnings of wisdom. He stopped in his traces to ask whether his life was making any sense. It is a question that all of us need to ask, and we can all sympathise with Arjuna in thinking that his present course of action was not sane, and that the answer might lie in the doctrine of quietism. After all, if one cannot act wisely, then at least it is better not actually to do harm. Better? Yes, but not the best. Inaction is after all the civil servant's way. It is true that you can't make a mistake if you do nothing. You can never, of course, be caught in the wrong. It is much safer to procrastinate and to say no. And one can always change one's mind, if it seems certain that one is right to do so, later, but meanwhile one has not actually made a positive mistake. Well, of course this policy does not really work. Life is a gamble. As the Bible said a long time ago, if one has a talent it is no good playing safe and burying it. It is no good simply putting it in the bank. We may lose it when we spend it, we may not create more with it, we have to take the risk, but it is the only way in fact of proceeding in life – to try and make something out of it.

Arjuna, then, is told by Shri Krishna that the policy of inaction will not do. The secret of wisdom, he says, is not to give up action at all, but to understand action and to act wisely. If a child has to learn to swim it must take the plunge. It must be willing to make mistakes. It is better to have tried and failed, than to have done nothing. Even the wise, says Shri Krishna, are bewildered about action and inaction. 'O Arjuna, one has to understand what action is, and likewise one has to understand what is wrong action. And one also has to understand about inaction. Hard to understand is the way of action.'[42] And he goes on to say

---

[42]*Bhagavad Gita* IV, 17.

something which is even more difficult to fathom: 'He who sees action in inaction, and sees inaction in action, he is wise among men. He is a Yogin and he has accomplished the object of all his action.'[43]

The first point that Shri Krishna makes, then, is that we have not to give up action – the doctrine of quietism will not do. It is a mistaken notion. And it is mistaken for two reasons. First, because it is impossible, and second, because it does not lead to the desired result. It is impossible because it is a chimera – a wrong idea. Man's nature is such that empirically his mind is a product of the energy of nature, and the energy of nature is nothing but activity. He can direct that activity, either outwardly or inwardly. He can decide in which direction he will focus his mind, but he cannot avoid this energy of the mind.

As it says in the *Gita*, there are two sides to man's nature. He is partly a product of nature, or *prakriti*, and partly he is a spirit, something beyond nature – he is the Self, the Divine Consciousness. But he is bound to follow his nature so long as he is an empirical being, and the mental side of his nature demands that he should act. And so, Krishna says, not by abstention from work does a man obtain freedom from action, nor by mere renunciation does he attain his perfection. For no one can remain for even a moment without doing work. Everyone is made to act helplessly by the impulses born of nature. 'He who restrains his organs of action imagining that he is being inactive, but continues in his mind to brood over the objects of sense, whose nature is deluded, is said to be a hypocrite. But he who controls the senses by the mind, and without attachment engages the organs of action in the path of work, he is a wise man. Do thou thy allotted work, for action is

---

[43] *Bhagavad Gita* IV, 18.

better than inaction. Even the maintenance of the physical life cannot be effected without action.'[44]

This, then, is the first great lesson that Shri Krishna gives Arjuna: that the secret of action is to act wisely, and that the real path for those who have this urge towards the spiritual Truth, is to direct the action on to another plane, to direct the action towards the restraining, as it says, of the sense organs, and the focussing of the mind. Action is often binding, but if one can understand the secret of action, then one can learn how to escape from its binding power.

One of the great modern Yogis, Swami Rama Tirtha, gives an illustration. He says that one of the great differences between people in the West and people in India, is the way that they eat. He says in the West people characteristically talk when they are eating and they do not pay much attention to the eating. Perhaps it is part of the puritan tradition in the West – I don't know if this is the explanation – but perhaps we think eating is rather a mundane pastime and not worthy of attention. But he says that the traditional attitude in India is that the food is taken in silence. People do not talk and they take it as a sacrament, in the traditional Hindu way, with a feeling that they are participating in a sacrament, and that they are, so to speak, taking into their own being part of the world of which they themselves form a part. So it has a religious and a spiritual connotation. And he also says that 'every process and every act of life, according to Vedanta, can be turned in this way into a spiritual act. When you are doing anything you should keep your thoughts always at home.'[45] What does he mean by keeping your thoughts always at home? It is to keep yourself always in what he calls your rightful centre. All action from the spiritual point

[44]*Bhagavad Gita* III, 5-9.

[45]Swami Rama Tirtha, *In Woods of God-Realization*, Vol 3.

of view, and also even from the subtle point of view, is done from a particular centre. And what really matters is the centre from which we act.

He says: 'Just as the fish live in the ocean of water, just as the birds live in the ocean of air, just so, you live in the ocean of light. In light you live, move and have your being.' He goes on to say – and it is an expression of the inner realisation of someone who was undoubtedly a master of Yoga, who had truly realised in his own experience what Yoga is about – 'Whether we are willing or unwilling, all the forces of Nature are bound to bring man to the realisation of Self. Favourable as well as unfavourable circumstances make no difference whatsoever. Just as in walking we raise one foot and then the other, pleasure and pain continually follow each other, and this process is working out throughout the whole universe. Those people are really happy who keep themselves above worldly pleasures and pains.'[46]

One is reminded in this passage of Swami Rama Tirtha's, of another verse from the second chapter of the *Gita*: 'To action alone thou hast a right, and never at all to its fruits. Let not the fruits of action be thy motive, neither let there be in thee any attachment to inaction.'[47] It's the same thing as Swami Rama Tirtha saying those people are really happy who keep themselves above worldly pleasures and pains. And he is saying that this is done by rising above the mind into this consciousness of the Light behind the mind, in which man lives, moves and has his being. In the enlightened man the situation, says Swami Rama Tirtha, is like that in a mature coconut. In the young coconut, if you try and break the shell the kernel is attached to the shell, and the kernel is also damaged. But in the mature coconut

---

[46]Swami Rama Tirtha, *In Woods of God-Realization*, Vol 3.

[47]*Bhagavad Gita* II, 47.

the kernel is detached from the shell, it is not attached to the husk. You can break it and it makes no difference to the kernel. So in the same way, if we can live not in the outer centre, the outer sphere, but contacting our real Life in this ocean of Light, then the outer circumstances will not be able to hurt us or impede us.

At this point we might meditate on this passage from Swami Rama Tirtha. It is not a meditation in the formal sense, but it is a quotation from his work:

> 'OM. JUST AS THE FISH LIVE IN THE OCEAN OF WATER, JUST AS THE BIRDS LIVE IN THE OCEAN OF AIR, JUST SO, I LIVE IN THE OCEAN OF LIGHT. IN LIGHT I LIVE, MOVE AND HAVE MY BEING. OM'

What matters then, according to Swami Rama Tirtha, is the centre from which we act.

Many years ago, I was in the Army for a short period doing National Service, in a War Office establishment a little way out of London and I commuted by train every day. One of the people I often travelled with was a retired colonel of the Army. He was a great character, a wonderful military figure, very correct, very polite with a real old-world courtesy. He was always completely immaculate, with the traditional bowler, pinstripe trousers, a very well rolled umbrella, and shoes I have never seen the like of, in which one could see the world reflected as in a shiny, limpid pool. I well remember the train often used to be very crowded. One night we were sitting in a compartment when somebody trod on the shoes of this figure, and I have never seen such a transformation. He very savagely kicked out at this man and was furious. This incident had an extraordinary impact, because it suddenly made one realise that here was someone who had something which was very vulnerable. He was completely, if you like, body centred, and for him the perfect appearance – the shining shoes – was his way of keeping what he believed himself to be as it should be and 'up to standard'. And, of course, it was very vulnerable.

Well, this is only an illustration, but it is an example of someone who acted, at least to a great extent, from an outer centre. His centre was the body – his appearance. We may not necessarily be body centred, but we still, in Swami Rama Tirtha's sense, may not have a true centre. Many people, for instance, have an exaggerated and inflamed egoity as the centre of their life. And as Swami Rama Tirtha says, it is like an exquisitely tender boil, and when someone threatens or touches that individuality, then they react somewhat like that colonel reacted in the compartment. They feel such pain when their ego is threatened that they could kill the person who has threatened it. Well, this again is not a true centre, it is not a centre from which one can act wisely. And one can see that here too the kernel of the coconut, so to speak, of the personality, is still very vulnerable – it is still attached to what is only a husk.

The ideal, says Swami Rama Tirtha, is to live like the bird on the branch. The bird sits on the branch and enjoys the branch, but it is not dependent on the branch. And if the branch is cut or blown down, then the bird flies off. This is the ideal. Of course, one lives in the body, and one lives with the ego, but not to make them any more of an obligatory abiding place, of an obligatory perch, than the bird makes of the branch – this is the secret, says Yoga, of wise action.

How then to escape the binding power of action? It is precisely this: it is to decouple the action from the individual self-interest, and there are various great ways of doing this.

One way which everyone, even the unspiritual, knows and appreciates, is the way of duty or *dharma* – to do something not because we particularly want to, not because it panders to any of our desires, but to do something because we know it is right and because it is our duty. The action for desire is no criterion for life. It does not bear thinking about as a way of having our whole life determined, all our actions determined. So the first and most empirical way, is action as *dharma* or duty. *Dharma*, say the spiritual classics, is the great upholder of society – it upholds them who uphold it – the great upholder of society and also of the individual. If one considers a policeman, often his duty must involve things he does not want to do, and which are unpleasant, but he does them. This is the ideal of *dharma*.

Implicit in the idea of duty, of course, is action done for the sake of something else, not for ourselves, action done for the sake of what is right. In other words, it is action done as service, whether it is service of an ideal, another individual, or a country or whatever it may be. But the big question in action done as service is what is that something to be for which it is done? Certainly one can see very great ideals in action. For instance, if you read Beethoven's letters or his testament, it is clear that for him his art was what he acted for. And in Beethoven one often gets the sense of how small he felt, how modest he was before the ideal of his art, and how impossible it was in his view ever to achieve what one should achieve for the sake of the art which he served. For St Teresa, it was the child Jesus which she used as a focus – a spiritual focus, high indeed, for which she did all that she did in her life.

The *Gita* says in chapter three: 'Save work done as and for a sacrifice, this world is in bondage to work, O Son of Kunti. Do thy work as a sacrifice, becoming free from all attachment.'[48] What do we mean by the word 'sacrifice'? It is action as an offering. Something which makes sacred, which makes what is offered holy. In other words, something which transmutes the dross of the most ordinary worldly act or object, provided it is offered in service and in love, into the gold of spiritual Light.

And the Lord later in the *Gita* is to say to Arjuna:

> 'Whosoever offers Me with devotion even a leaf, a flower, a fruit, or even water, that offering of love of the pure heart I accept. Whatever thou doest, whatever thou eatest, whatever thou givest away, whatever austerity thou dost practice, do that, O Son of Kunti, as an offering to Me. Thus shalt thou be freed from the good and evil results which are the bonds of action. With thy mind firmly set on the way of renunciation, thou shalt become free and attain to Me.'[49]

The offering is the outer form, but self-giving is what matters. This is the common element in all sacrifices, great and small, giving a bit of ourselves, of what is our own, in service. And, of course, says the *Gita*, in this sense the whole of life can be made into an offering, because our thought and our action is also creative, and in this way we make the centre from which we think and act, the focus towards which we direct our thought and action, the determinants of the quality of our life – we can make these. We can transmute our life, simply by the focus that we have for our action and our thought. People talk a great deal nowadays about improving the quality of life. Well, the Yogis would say that the most effective way of improving the quality of life is to have the right centre to act from and the right focus for action.

---

[48] *Bhagavad Gita* III, 9.
[49] *Bhagavad Gita* IX, 27 and 28.

One is reminded in our own tradition of that wonderful line in the *Book of Common Prayer*: 'O God, whose service is perfect freedom.'[50] The *Gita* stresses this point again and again: that Karma Yoga, the secret of right action as an offering to the Lord – the highest ideal – is the means to attain the right centre and the right focus for action.

One can illustrate this finally and most easily, by taking the extreme beginning of the *Gita* and the extreme end. At the beginning this point is made and at the end the work comes back to it. At the beginning in verse 44 of chapter two: 'The intelligence (the mind) which is to be trained, of those who are devoted to enjoyment and power, and whose minds are carried away by the words of the Veda promising them heaven, is not concentrated and is not centred in the Self.' It is not focussed – it has not got a focus and it is not centred in the Self. In the last verses of chapter eighteen the final message Shri Krishna gives to Arjuna is this:[51]

> 'Doing continually all actions whatsoever taking refuge in Me, by My Grace he reaches the Eternal, Undecaying Abode. Mentally offering all deeds to Me, regarding Me as the Supreme, resorting to mental concentration do thou ever fix thy heart on Me. Fixing thy heart on Me thou shalt by My Grace cross over all difficulties.'

---

[50]Morning Prayer, *Book of Common Prayer*.

[51]*Bhagavad Gita* XVIII, 56–58.

9

The Property of Selfhood*

IN SOME SENSES we are all concerned one way or another with the problems of owning property, and the whole of human history revolves round these problems: what it means to own property, what should be the case, and so forth. Particularly, one might say, in the last hundred years man has been politically and economically preoccupied with the question of the division of wealth and the inequalities and injustices to which it gives rise.

But the spiritual teachers also have something to say on this topic and it is in some ways more revolutionary than the most radical of economic doctrines or political theories. So let us remind ourselves of some of the ideas which mankind has had about property through the ages, some of the great philosophical ideas, and then, in the light of these ideas, let us look at what the great spiritual teachers have said on this matter.

As a starting point, let us take the verses in the sixteenth chapter of the *Bhagavad Gita* which speak of the spiritually blind and unregenerate man. A contrast is made between the spiritual man and the unregenerate man, about whom we have the verses:

> 'Bound by hundreds of bands of hope, given over to lust and wrath, they strive to secure, by unjust

*A lecture given on 11th March 1966.

> means, hoards of wealth for sensual enjoyment.' (Verse 12)
>
> 'This today has been gained by me; this desire I shall attain tomorrow; this is mine now, and this wealth also shall be mine in the future.' (Verse 13)
>
> 'I am rich and well-born. Who else is equal to me?' (Verse 15)

These verses of the *Gita* describe the attitude or ideas typical of the worldling and it is clear from them that they represent the desire to amass wealth. Evidently then, the desire to amass wealth, to gain domination over all others, is at least one characteristic of those who are unspiritual, those who are deluded and lack spiritual wisdom.

There is, of course, a steady stream of thought among the great philosophers, particularly among the idealists, who in the course of human history have advocated the abolition of all wealth or the institution of a social order in which there should be no property. Not only among philosophers, we also find, of course, many of the saints who gave up great wealth to become beggars and monks in order to teach mankind spiritually. One has only to remember Prince Sikhidwaja in *Yoga Vasishtha* who gave up a kingdom to seek Self-Realization, as did Prince Siddhartha to become the Buddha, St Francis who gave up his very rich family and aristocratic background to become the greatest of the medieval saints of the Christian Church, and many others like St Thomas Aquinas. In the yogic tradition in our own time Shri Dada of Aligarh gave up his family wealth.

And yet, equally, one finds that some of the greatest spiritual figures have been and have remained very wealthy rulers, like King Janaka in the Upanishadic times, King

Shivaji, Mohammed and King Ashoka, to mention only a few.

In our own Christian tradition we find that Christ on the one hand told one of his disciples: 'Give all you have to the poor and follow Me'. On the other hand, He said: 'I come that ye shall have life and have it more abundantly.' 'Seek ye first the Kingdom of Heaven and all else shall be added unto you.' There was no need for Him to have added the second clause; He could very well have said: 'Seek ye first the Kingdom of Heaven because My Kingdom is not of this world.' But, in fact, He didn't choose to say this. This is what He chose to say: 'I come that ye shall have life and have it more abundantly.' So there is a mystery here, something which needs thinking about, which is not at first obvious and something, in fact, which we have to think about deeply if we are to understand fully or even partially what the spiritual teaching is.

Going back for a minute to those who have been concerned in the past not with spiritual methods but with establishing the perfect worldly society, there have been, as has been mentioned, some among these who believed that it was only necessary to abolish all private property in order to bring Utopia. One hasn't to go forward as far as Karl Marx to find this; even in ancient Greece Pythagoras, long before Plato, founded a society in which all property was held in common and there was a common way of life. We are accustomed to consider ourselves very advanced nowadays in the matter of the emancipation of women, but in Pythagorean society men and women were admitted on equal terms. The society was devoted to science and mathematics and music particularly; even the discoveries which were made were considered not to be made by individuals but to be the result of collective effort.

What Pythagoras thought about commerce and amassing wealth is probably very well illustrated by his description of the three sorts of people which he thought there were in the world. He said the world was full of three sorts of people who were like the three sorts of people who came to the Olympic Games. There was a middling sort that came to compete in the games; there was a superior sort that came only to watch the games; and there was an inferior sort who came only to buy and sell. It's not clear whether he would have the same view about those who go to watch football in the present age. But what he was really thinking about when he said that the superior class were those who simply went to watch the games was that the disinterested non-competitive attitude of the scientist or the philosopher was superior to the competitive attitude of the person who was competing in the games.

Later, in Greece, Plato in his conception of the ideal society, described in his most famous book the *Republic*, put the government in the hands of what he called the guardians, the small section of society who were meant to be philosopher-sages. And again he insisted that they should hold no private property and that they were forbidden to touch gold and silver. They were to live together in small houses, eating simple food in a common dining room, and both women and men could become guardians and were to have complete equality.

Well, these are all very well as theoretical ideas but Plato quite clearly recognised that human nature might be too much for him, for even without the opportunity to own property or to amass wealth, private possessive emotions can still find an outlet, and of course the most obvious outlet is in the family. Plato was a very radical thinker and he wasn't put off by this. He said that the solution was that all children were to be removed at birth, that no child was to be told who his parents were and that all children were to call each other brother and sister, or when they were addressing older people, father and mother. Well, this is a very philosophical solution. But it is interesting that this was seriously put forward. I think it's quite clear that there would have been great difficulties if Plato's plan had ever been put into operation, particularly when a young woman had to address another woman, as to whether to call her 'mother' or 'sister', but Plato does not mention this difficulty. Though very logical and though he quite clearly thought about this problem deeply, Plato's plan looks to us very like the most unpleasant sort of totalitarian state, even though it is entirely benevolent in its objectives. And though he values justice very highly and his aim is to beget human happiness, it's quite clear that human freedom is not very well provided for in the *Republic*.

There are many other great figures, as you know, who subsequently thought about this problem - Rousseau, Tolstoy and Marx, for instance, all believed that property should be abolished. But they all tried to solve it by an externally imposed solution. There is a problem of inequality in property, there is no question. Everyone must admit this, whether they believe in the principle of equality or not. But all these proposals try to solve the problem by externally imposed solutions, without curing it at the source. As Christ said, it was not that which came from without which defiled a man but the things which proceeded from within, from the heart of man: evil thoughts, thefts, dishonesty and the rest. And the question in view evidently is that an externally imposed solution, to try and get rid of the selfish individualistic impulses in man which lead to inequality and lead to social injustice, is not effective. One has to solve the problem by tackling it at its source, in the heart of man.

There is, of course, another difficulty about an external solution. It aims to impose equality on society. But you cannot make all men equal in their aptitudes and their gifts. The essence of nature is multiplicity, the thousand variations that it produces on a single theme. Rousseau recognised this when he distinguished between natural inequalities and artificial inequalities. He held that natural inequalities between man and man, for instance between age or between health or intelligence, were not bad. What was bad was solely the artificial inequalities which resulted from privilege and were authorised by social convention. For him society was the root of all evil and this had its origin in private property. This was the cause in its turn of all the unnatural social inequalities which were so marked in his day. 'The first man,' he says, 'who having enclosed a piece of land, bethought himself of saying "this is mine" and found people simple enough to believe him, was the real founder of civil society.' To undo this evil Rousseau thought it was only necessary to abandon civilisation – a pretty drastic solution, one would think!

Anyway this is only one side of the argument. In fact, Rousseau sent his contemporary, Voltaire, a copy of his first book[52] on this subject. Voltaire already radically disagreed with Rousseau, believing that property, far from being evil, was a good influence on mankind for he said it made a man responsible and 'doubled a man's strength'. It was certain, said Voltaire, that a man would cultivate and look after what he owned far better than he would look after something belonging to somebody else. It is a truth that modern Communist states are having to learn by

---

[52]*The Social Contract - or Principles of Political Right* by Jean Jacques Rousseau 1762 Translated 1782 by G. D. H. Cole, public domain.

degrees. And the great problem in these experiments is that of motivation. We know this well enough surely from the Civil Service. Anyway, Voltaire wrote back to Rousseau:

> 'I have received your new book against the human race, and thank you for it. Never was such cleverness used in the design of making us all stupid. One longs, in reading your book, to walk on all fours. But as I have lost that habit for more than sixty years, I feel unhappily the impossibility of resuming it. Nor can I embark in search of the savages of Canada, because the maladies to which I am condemned render a European surgeon necessary to me; because war is going on in those regions; and because the example of our actions has made the savages nearly as bad as ourselves.'[53]

Well, we need not follow the history of ideas about private property and the organisation of society through the great seventeenth and eighteenth century thinkers, Locke and Hume, down to the Utilitarians and Karl Marx. But suffice it to say that those, like Marx, who have advocated the abolition of private property have always done so on the grounds that, if you have it, you give free play to human selfishness and exploitation. You then get inequalities of class and the exploitation of the 'have-nots' by the 'haves'.

Now, it is equally clear that many spiritual teachers have also emphasised this, but with a major difference. They have always sought to persuade, or to convert people by the power of love and benevolence and truth, and they have never sought – at least the greatest of them and the best of them – to coerce their fellowmen by force. St

[53]Voltaire, *Correspondence*, Institut et Musee Voltaire, 1953.

Francis preached the doctrine of spiritual poverty in an age when the Church was the wealthiest organisation in society. Another saint, John Wycliffe, in fourteenth century England, who gave up his post as a leading teacher in the University of Oxford to become a poor parish priest for the last ten years of his life, also spoke out against the wealth of the Church and against the inequalities that it had led to. His medium was sympathy with the poor and a disgust for the rich and very worldly ecclesiastics of his time. He instituted the teaching friars who went out to the poor with a special mission and, in fact, he inspired not only people in England but also the great Protestant movement of Huss in Eastern Europe of that time. A great reform movement within the Church was started by Wycliffe. He was also, of course, the man who, in order to make the Bible available to the ordinary people, was the first to translate it into the vernacular, into English.

In Russia, nearer our own day, Tolstoy was one of the great figures. The inspirer of Mahatma Gandhi in India, strangely enough, was not initially the Indian teaching, the Vedanta teaching, but it was Tolstoy. Gandhi was converted to his ideas by Tolstoy, whom he read as a young man, and it was Tolstoy's teaching about property and the state which made Gandhi into what he was. Tolstoy didn't believe in revolution but he made one important point which goes further than many of the philosophers. I quote you just a short passage from Tolstoy. He says:[54]

> 'Today possessions are the root of all evil; they cause the suffering of those who possess and of those who do not possess, and the danger of collision is unavoidable

[54]Stefan Zweig - *Stefan Zweig Presents the Living Thoughts of Tolstoi* – The Living Thoughts Library 3rd Edition 1945.

> between those who have too much and those who live in poverty. All evil begins with property and so long as the state still recognises the principle of property, it is the chief of the guilty parties.'

He goes on to say that wars and commerce and many of the other features of the State are all based on property. Tolstoy preached, of course, really again, the abolition of property and the abolition of the State, rather as Rousseau had. And his solution was that the property owning classes, spoilt children of culture, and the pauper classes can be reconciled only if the property owning classes voluntarily give up their privileges and cease to make such great demands upon life.[55]

> 'Let the rich man give up his wealth, the intellectual his arrogance. Let the artist create his works, with a view solely to intelligibility for the masses; let everyone live wholly by his own work, receiving no more for it than he needs for this primitive form of life.'

This, then, is Tolstoy's central idea – social levelling by the voluntary giving up of property. But he does make one important point, which is not made by the other philosophers, that wealth is just as bad for the wealthy as it is for the poor. The tacit assumption in the other philosophers is that it is the rich who are to be envied and the poor who are to be pitied as unlucky and this assumption needs questioning. Is it really so? Without going to the spiritual teachers, we all know if we think about it that it isn't so, and that it is just as possible to be miserable and suffering on a hundred thousand pounds a year as it is with sixpence in one's pocket. Surely, the songs, the literature and the drama of

---

[55]Stefan Zweig - *Stefan Zweig Presents the Living Thoughts of Tolstoi* – The Living Thoughts Library 3rd Edition 1945.

mankind are full of instances and statements of this fact. Not only Shakespeare's 'Uneasy lies the head that wears the crown'[56] and many other passages, but we also have the story of the unhappy king who went to a sage and asked how to become happy. The sage told him that he could only become happy if he could wear the shirt of a happy man. And you know that after a long search he found a happy man but the man was so poor he had no shirt. Well, we don't imagine that those like Clore or Gulbenkian, who lie awake at night worrying about where their next million is going to come from, are happier than we are. Or if we do imagine it, then we are very foolish.

The fact is that the acquisitive, proprietary propensities of the human mind have a long history, much longer even than any of these philosophers have realised. They can be clearly seen at work even in the prehuman stages of evolution. We only have to watch a dog owning and protecting the bone which it has acquired, or consider the bird, who defends its territory against trespassers, with all the enthusiasm of a medieval landowner. Animals will always protect their own young, regarding them as something that is both precious and peculiarly their own, in a way which suggests that Plato's plans for the *Republic* are doomed even before they have been tried out!

So perhaps the theorists and the thinkers and the philosophers who advocate the abolition of property are a little out of touch with the realities of the world they live in and the human nature which they are trying to deal with. In this case it is worth looking at what the spiritual teachers have to say, to see if perhaps they have something more profound or more important to offer. The teaching of Yoga is that, all that we call 'mine' – all our property –

---

[56]Shakespeare's *Henry IV. Part II*, 1597.

is an arbitrary extension of our own ego. It is simply part of what we feel identified with. Its arbitrariness is obvious because when we try to decide what it consists of or where its boundaries are, they change from moment to moment as we think about it. They change with whatever we feel them to be. Not only is this true of the boundaries of what we call 'mine' but there is an equal difficulty, the Yogis point out to us, about deciding the nature of the owner of the property, of the 'I'. In one sense, we seem to have two things: we seem to have an owner, 'I', and his possessions, what he calls 'mine'. These are clearly distinct, like a king and his kingdom. But what we feel to be 'I' changes from moment to moment and often includes at one time much that we think of as 'mine' at another time.

Let us first take the simplest example before we come to the more complicated ones. The arbitrariness of property is very well seen in the problems we have in dealing with the world outside, dividing the world outside, for example in the last few years, the great controversies about territorial waters. How far does one territorial water go and can one get agreement about it? It's very difficult. What about territorial claims? There is a company in America which has already sold plots of land on the moon. Well, what about the claims of the people who have staked out and bought parts of the moon? It's quite clear that, as in the case of territorial waters, so in the case of the moon plots, these claims can only have any validity by consent. In fact, we are back in the rule of law to the realm of something which is arbitrary and which we can only accept if everybody agrees about it. Those who know or read Locke will know that Locke says that this is the basis of society, the social contract, whether one believes in a social contract or not. As Hume says, it's just a feeling, it's not a formal contract, it's still a question of consent, only of consent.

These examples of arbitrariness in deciding the limits of what belongs to oneself or one's nation are trivial compared with those we meet when we come to ask what is the meaning of 'I' and 'mine'. Our house is clearly a part of what we call 'mine' and not 'I', but what about our clothes? Sometimes we feel our clothes as 'I', as part of ourself, and our body we certainly feel much more often as 'I'. When it comes to our nails, perhaps they are 'I' until we cut them, or our hair. But even here we have times when we feel them to be mine and times when we feel them to be ourself.

It is still more difficult to decide about the mind, about our feelings and ideas and sensations, our reason and our will. Are these part of what we own, are they part of our property or are they part of ourself? According to Vedanta, according to the yogic teachings, all this is part of our possessions. These are our instruments and not our real Self. It is part of what we own, if you like, or part of what we feel we own, part of the objects of experience, part of the 'this' which presents itself before us in experience. The acquisitive ego in man, when it is spiritually blind, seeks to extend its wealth and possessions and to dominate and annex as much of the world as it can. As the *Gita* verse says, it wants as much as possible of what is felt to be other than itself, what is felt to be 'not-I', to become 'mine', to be in some sense identified with itself. But this ego, say the Yogis, is not the real Self of man at all but is an impostor. It is this ego which says, in the words quoted earlier from the *Gita*: 'This I will acquire today; that I will acquire tomorrow.'[57] The more successful it seems to be in this, the more deluded and the more of a nuisance it becomes. For these things, this 'wealth amassed for sensual enjoyment', as the *Gita* says, do not bring it happiness, and its appetite for more is as insatiable as its dissatisfaction and its darkness.

---

[57] *Bhagavad Gita* XVI, 13

We have surely seen the careers of enough dictators in the world to see which way this path leads. Alexander, Napoleon, Ghengis Khan, Tamburlaine, Hitler, Stalin – not one achieved happiness in the sense that the great saints achieved it.

When Christ says: 'It is easier for a camel to go through the eye of a needle, than for a rich man to enter the Kingdom of Heaven',[58] the main problem does not seem to be the smallness of the eye of the needle, but the inflated size of the 'I' of most rich men! There is a real sense, according to the spiritual teachers, in which possessions, in which enlarging the realm of the 'mine' and intensifying the feeling of possession and power and domination, are a real limitation on the soul of man. One of our great modern scientists, Albert Einstein, once said very wisely: 'All possessions are like stones tied to your legs.' In other words, what he meant was that possessions are a limitation. And a great secret taught by the spiritual teachers is that man, to be free and to be wise, needs to achieve independence of possessions, independence of outer objects, independence of the body and finally independence of the mind through knowledge and through renunciation. One of the great modern Yogis, Swami Rama Tirtha, has a poem:[59]

> 'My heart is set on asceticism;
> Carrying my staff and manuscript under my arm
> I am ruler of half the world.
> I live on crusts given me as alms,
> But I walk abroad like a rich man.
> O Rama, the joy of the companionship of God
> Far exceeds the delight of kingship.'

Does this ideal mean giving up everything? It means depending on one's own higher Self, the higher Self which rules the

[58] Matthew 19:24; Mark 10:25; Luke 18:25

[59] Swami Rama Tirtha, *In Woods of God-Realization*, Vol 3.

universe, according to the great Yogis. 'Seek ye first the Kingdom of Heaven and the rest shall be added unto you.'[60]

There is the example from the life of the holy Prophet Mohammed of Abu Bakr, a very rich man who was the first to convert to Mohammed's teaching and then gave up all his great wealth to the prophet and thereafter the prophet gave it back to him in trust. He said: 'Abu Bakr, keep it in trust and use it for the good of all mankind and in the propagation of the spiritual teachings.' Abu Bakr showed his independence of his possessions, his willingness to give them up.

Swami Rama Tirtha gives another example. He says that the spiritually wise man is like a bird, sitting on the branch of a tree. He may through his past karma find himself a rich man or a poor man or in any branch of society. In that role in society he will use what means there are for the welfare of all with whom he comes in contact, for the good of all beings. But he is like the bird on a branch. If the branch breaks, then he simply flies away. He is not dependent on it. If it is there, he sits on it; if it isn't there, then he is not dependent on it. And in this sense, to become independent is the spiritual teaching – of possessions, of the body, of the mind and so on. And then the promise of the Lord in the *Gita* is: 'O Arjuna, for my devotees I protect what they have and provide what they need.'[61] It is the same message that Christ gave His disciples when He said: 'Consider the lilies of the field; they toil not, neither do they spin.'[62] God would provide for them just as He provided for the lilies.

Real renunciation in the spiritual sense comes only through Knowledge. The real abolition, if you like, of property, of which the thinkers speak, the philosophers speak, is not the

---

[60]Matthew 6:33

[61]*Bhagavad Gita* IX, 22.

[62]Luke 12:32, Matthew 6:25-34

abolition of the outer property. It is to abolish the false ego created by the mind through Knowledge, to give up the sense of possession of the mind, which is the root of all selfishness and unspirituality. When the sense of 'me' and 'mine' can be given up, say the Yogis, then a man is spiritually awakened.

10

Breaking the Idol*

IN HIS BOOK *Psychoanalysis and Religion*, the American psychologist Erich Fromm gives a very graphic statement, I think, of what a Western psychologist, a thinking person, feels about man's present situation. That though things may be very well materially in Western civilisation, with regard to the mind of man, with regard to inner peace, happiness and satisfaction, things are anything but well.

Man is subject to a deep neurosis and perhaps neurotic illness is much more prevalent among the so-called welfare states, the rich well-to-do modern civilisations, than it is in the simpler civilisations, the so-called more primitive civilisations. Fromm, then, makes this first important point that man is deeply subject to neurosis, and he points out that there is a connection between man's religious needs, his spiritual needs, and this neurosis. The connection was originally made by Freud. We may not entirely agree with Freud's teaching, but he was undoubtedly a great pioneer in the field of psychology with many insights into the mind. As you know, Freud's view was that religion was the communal neurosis of mankind. Fromm, now an influential figure in American psychology, rejects this view. He says that, on the contrary, when one examines the question, though it's perfectly true that neurosis concerns the religious questions, neurosis itself is a return to a primitive, inadequate condition

*A lecture given on 2nd July 1965.

which is due to the religious needs of man not being met. Religion and neurosis have perhaps a great connection in this way.

'Neurosis, we can say, is a symptom of the failure of the individual to achieve psychological maturity. This is the definition the psychologists give: the failure of the individual to achieve psychological maturity, the failure to achieve independence of the personality and to accomplish the aims which every man desires, the aims which make him truly a human being, to be creative in his life, to live with love in his life, and to think truly.' This is what Fromm says. Anyone who has failed to achieve maturity and integration develops a neurosis of one kind or another. He doesn't just live unbothered by this failure, satisfied to eat, drink, sleep and do his work. If this were the case then we would indeed have proof that the religious attitude, while perhaps desirable, is not an intrinsic part of human nature. But the study of man shows that this is not so.

If a person has not succeeded in integrating his energies in the direction of his higher Self, he canalises them in the direction of lower goals. If he has no picture of the world and his position in it which approximates to the truth, he will create a picture which is illusory and he will cling to it with the same tenacity with which a religionist believes in his beliefs, his creed. Indeed man does not live by bread alone. He has only the choice of better or worse, higher or lower, satisfactory or destructive forms of religions and philosophies.

Fromm is saying, then, that intrinsic in the nature of man, in the very essence of human nature as it is in the human mind, there are religious needs which have to be met and if they are not met, then man pays the consequence in neurosis. He says that man is not free to choose between having or not having ideals but is only free to choose between different kinds of ideals, for instance, between being devoted to power and destruction or being devoted to reason and love. Each and every man is in this sense an idealist, and each and every man is by his nature striving for something beyond the attainment of the merely physical satisfactions of food and sense pleasure. They may differ in the kind of ideals they believe in, but deep in human nature this need is there and it does find some sort of outlet.

This is a very cogent statement by someone who has nothing to do with the Yoga tradition, but is a Western psychologist, trained in the Freudian tradition, practising psychoanalysis in America. We can see, then, that the view even here is that worship is not either exclusively or specifically a religious activity. It is a natural and inevitable activity of the human mind, whether we recognise it or not. It may, of course, have a special significance in a religious context, but it is not specifically religious. It is human – it is simply something that man does and must do. Man can worship animals, trees, idols of stone or gold, an invisible God, a saintly man or a diabolical leader, as he did in the Germany of the 1930s. He may worship his ancestors, his nation, his class or party, money or success. His religion in this sense may be conducive to the development of destructiveness or of love, of domination or of brotherliness. It may further his power of reason or it may paralyse it. He may be aware of his system as being religious, different from the beliefs in the secular realm, or he may think that he has no religion and may simply interpret his idealism, his devotion to certain allegedly secular aims, like power, money and success, as nothing but his concern for the practical and the expedient. The question is not 'religion or not', but which kind of religion, whether it is one furthering man's development, the unfolding of his human potentialities, or one paralysing them.

We can say that the mind is in a sense a natural idolater. We tend to forget that idolatry is not only the worship of this or that particular idol, but it is also a human attitude and a very common human attitude. We may ask: what do we mean by idolatry? We can say that idolatry is the deification of things, of partial aspects of things, as if they were the whole, as if they were the only thing that really mattered, and the submission of the individual's mind to that thing which has been deified. Idolatry in this sense is in contrast to the attitude of the mind in which life is devoted to the realisation of the highest principles of love and reason, of tolerance and universality, and also the attitude of becoming what man potentially is: a being made in the likeness of God. It isn't only figures in stone or pictures which can be idols; ideas can be idols, words can be idols, leaders, the state, even science can be an idol and so can public opinion, the opinion of one's neighbours, and God has become an idol for many, Fromm says.

These are very interesting and very profound points which Fromm makes. It is evident that in this idolatry of the human mind the quality of the thing which we worship, the quality of the thing we make an idol in our mind, the thing to which we give supreme value, is a very important determinant of our life. But not only that, not only the quality of the thing itself, but also the quality of our attitude towards it can make it either good or bad, according to that attitude.

Even God has become an idol for many, says Fromm. Well, we can ask: how can God become an idol? Surely, God, a universal being, the ruler of the universe, becomes an idol in those religions when ideas of narrowness are connected with Him: the idea that God has one chosen people and that all others are heathen. The Calvinist idea that God has predestined a certain section of humanity to be the elect and that all who have not been so predestined are doomed to eternal punishment. These surely are making idols of God.

There is a Zen story of a Buddhist who built a temple and had a statue of Buddha put there. But the other Buddhists came and they also had statues of the Buddha which they wanted to put up. He used to go every day to burn incense in front of his Buddha, but he began to notice that when he burnt the incense, the smoke spread out and went in front of the other Buddhas as well. This displeased him very much because it was to his Buddha that he wished to burn the incense. So after some time he bought a special burner with a funnel which led the smoke up so that it was only released just below the head of the Buddha. Gradually, the face of the Buddha turned black and it became known as the black-nosed Buddha. Well, this is the story. If the spirit of narrowness comes into the worship, if we want to make God simply our God and nobody else's God, then God has become an idol and we are idolaters.

What, then, does Yoga say? So far, this is just an idea of what we can see as the conclusions from Western psychologists. What does Yoga say on this point? Well, something very surprising, which shouldn't be over interpreted or any conclusion jumped to too quickly. But we can say from one point of view, let's say from the highest point of view, from the point of view of the spiritual truth, Yoga says that all worship of God is idolatry. This sounds a very strange statement. I shall have to try and defend this statement. Let us start by quoting the *Kena Upanishad.* These are some verses from one of the oldest classics of

Yoga: 'That which is not expressed through speech but by which speech is expressed, that, verily, know thou as the absolute God and not what people worship here. That which is not thought by the mind but by which it is said the mind thinks, that, verily, know thou as the absolute God and not what people here adore in worship.'

If we come to the Western tradition, and we take one of the very greatest of the Western mystics, Meister Eckhart, we find that he too held that the pure Godhead, the ultimate, the absolute God, was beyond all conceiving by the mind. The mind can't conceive of God. Any ideas that we can have of God, that reality, says Eckhart, are idols; this is the word he uses. Any ideas that the mind can have of God in the empirical realm are idols. 'Had I a God whom I could understand intellectually,' says Eckhart, 'I would no longer hold Him for God.'[63] Had I a God whom I could understand *with my mind,* I would no longer hold Him for God. Eckhart didn't believe that God was unknowable. On the contrary, he believed that through mystical experience He could be known. He says: 'When the soul beholds God purely, it takes all its being and its life and whatever it is from the depth of God and knows nothing but only to be with God. So soon as it becomes conscious that it sees and loves and knows God, that is in itself a departure.'

So the teaching of Eckhart, which is the same as the teaching of Yoga here, is that while knowledge is in the mind, in the realm of the intellect, it is indirect knowledge, and it has to be knowledge through an image or a symbol. Only direct knowledge takes us beyond idolatry. Only direct knowledge takes us to the knowledge of the thing in itself. And this is only possible in what the Yogis call illumination or enlightenment. So that all worship is in terms of images in the mind or ideas.

---

[63]Meister Eckhart, Sermon 83, 207.

One of the great modern Yogis, Swami Rama Tirtha, asks in his article on worship, translated by our teacher, Dr Shastri, and published by Shanti Sadan in the book *Scientist and Mahatma*: 'What is an image that we worship? The root meaning of the Sanskrit word for image *pratima* is a "unit of measurement". Thus every image is a unit by which we measure God.' According to Yoga, the mind is a finitising principle, something which limits our vision, which limits the reality. It can think only in the finite categories of time and space, the relationships of time and space, and causation. To handle the immeasurable reality of God, it has to make that reality measurable. It must cut it down, so to speak, into some manageable size. It is like a child who, when you give him a sum in arithmetic to work out, can't do the sum in his head. He has to do it by transforming the sum into the beads on an abacus. By analogy, the mind is in the same position in thinking about reality. But there is of course a great danger in this process, a great danger against which Swami Rama Tirtha warns us. We must not take the image or the symbol for the reality. We must not imagine that in using a small and insignificant image we are really reducing the reality to insignificance.

The reduction, the use of a symbol for worship at all is a concession, not in the reality, but a concession to our mind, because we too in this respect are children. Spiritually, we are children before we have the direct knowledge of the sages. Just as the incarnation itself, God made man in the Christian doctrine, was a concession to the inability of mankind at large to rise to the transcendent spiritual reality unaided, so through images and symbols the great spiritual teachers bring the reality, the truth, down into the realm where we can approach it and understand it. We can say the mind is continually substituting an image for the real thing, not only in spiritual matters but also even in ordinary matters. And one of the reasons why the mind is such an unreliable guide and such a deceiver, is that it is continually presenting to us an image as the real thing and continually attributing to the real thing the qualities of the image. How often our ideas, even about other people, are really a façade that we have created, an image that we have created, and we find on closer examination or through some experience that people are quite different from what we had imagined firmly in our mind that they were. This is a quality of the mind, to deceive us about things.

We can say, then, that the narrowness in religion is put there not by the teachings themselves but by the distortions introduced into them by the mind of man. One of the great points which the teacher of our teacher, Shri Dadaji, inculcated into all his pupils was the spirit of universality, that real spirituality implied a spirit of universality. He said that there is no real contradiction in the core of truth, although the paths to that truth, the paths by which people approach that truth, may be varied.

The different symbols used in different religions are simply different means to one and the same end. When some of his Hindu disciples erected a temple in Moradabad, he told them that while the temple was indeed a good thing to have built, it was not the true temple. The true temple, of which the outer one was only a symbol, was the invisible temple which is to be built by each and every man within his own heart. The same God, worshipped as Shiva in the Hindu temple, said Shri Dada, as Allah in the Mohammedan mosque, and as Jesus in the Christian church, is enshrined within that inner temple in the heart in each and every man, and no special creed or prayer is God's particular creed or particular prayer.

God is universal. He is universally present because there is no man who hasn't this divine element within his own being. 'I abide deep in the hearts of all beings'[64], says the Lord in the *Bhagavad Gita*. And Shri Dada advised his disciples: 'From visible worship proceed to invisible worship, from the particular pass to the universal. Transcend creed and dogma by reverence for the Absolute who has no names and yet responds to any name by which you call on Him with sincerity and love.' Symbols are not bad in themselves, then, according to the yogic doctrine, but they become impediments if we take them for that which is symbolised and remain content in their limitations.

It is interesting to compare the attitude of the different religions in this sphere. As you know, you can go into a mosque and you won't find any statues or any pictures of any kind. The reason for this is that Mohammed laid down that it was impious to try and make any representation of God, any representation of spiritual truths, spiritual reality, because it was beyond man's power to represent them pictorially. How different, one may say, from the Hindu or the Christian art where this tradition wasn't followed and where one has wonderful works of art, very great works of art, used to represent. But those attitudes are extremes. There is nothing wrong in the symbol, but we haven't got to take the symbol for the reality. We haven't got to take even the picture by Rubens or Leonardo or Tintoretto as the reality – it's simply a symbol, an image.

In the Chinese tradition one has something which is perhaps neither of these. There they do express spiritual themes in pictures, in the Zen pictures for instance, but it's only by hinting. The tradition is never to represent fully but only to hint at the spiritual truth. This is again another way of trying to use symbols to represent the truth.

One can say, then, that many different traditions exist which have tried to use symbols in different ways, but

---

[64] *Bhagavad Gita* X, 20; XIII, 17; XV, 15 and XVIII, 61.

the fact remains that the symbol and the symbolised are not the same and that one mustn't attribute to the symbolised the limitations of the symbol.

In the Vedanta, in the yogic tradition, following the *Kena Upanishad*, there is a recognition of the value of the symbol but also of the importance of reminding the worshipper that it is different from the symbolised. Those who want to follow the subject further are recommended to read the chapter on the symbol and the symbolised in the book by Marjorie Waterhouse *Training the Mind through Yoga* published by Shanti Sadan. In the *Brahma Sutras* when it speaks of worship, it says: 'The symbol is to be viewed as if it were God, but God is not to be viewed as if He were the symbol.' It is a very important and subtle difference.

Man must remember, the yogis remind us, that any idea that he has of the spiritual reality before he has direct knowledge of it, is only a symbol and falls far short of it. It is interesting that an opera by Schönberg has recently been produced at Covent Garden, called *Moses and Aaron*, which is on precisely this theme. This was Schönberg's great but unfinished opera – in which he compares and contrasts Moses and his brother Aaron in their teaching of the children of Israel. Moses, the sage, has real access to spiritual experience. He has ascended Mount Sinai and seen God face to face. He knows the truth but because he knows it he finds it impossible, or finds it very difficult, to express it in terms which the people can understand. Aaron then says, well, I'll teach the people and he makes the symbol, but his symbol turns into something much too concrete and the end of Aaron's teaching is the fatted calf, the golden calf. It is the age-old problem of the spiritual paths: when the real truth which is transcendental, is forgotten, when it is falsified and open to misinterpretation, when it is made easy and into something concrete for the mind, then religion degenerates into superstition and into materialism.

There is, however, another line of thought which is also an aspect of the yogic teaching – there is a very great idol, the greatest idol that man worships, and that idol is his own ego. And it is a false worship in precisely the same way. You may remember Rodin has a statue of a man kneeling before a woman and he calls it the eternal idol. But really this is not the eternal idol for all mankind. A much greater idol, more universally worshipped than this idol, is the ego. He should have made a statue of the ego of man because, at some time in his career, there is no individual who does not worship his ego. The personality of man, then, is an idol; it is a symbol of the real Self. It is not the real Self at all. It is a finite entity, created by the mind, and it is no less of an image than any of his other images. Even the name that we have, 'the personality', comes from the Old Greek *persona* which literally meant the mask which was worn by the actor during the Greek plays. The personality is really a mask, a mask which is worn by the individual in his mind, the mask created by the mind. If man remains worshipping this personality, the ego, as if it were his real Self, then he eventually becomes lost in narrowness and in error. This is what Yoga calls the bondage of ignorance because the real 'I' of man, the real Self of man, is something much greater than the mind, is something much greater than the emotions or than the instincts, or than even the intellect. It is a spiritual reality, a reality behind the mind.

There is a story of another Zen traveller, a Zen Master, going to a temple on a cold winter's day where there were some statues of Buddha, as in the other temple, and since he was cold, he took one of the statues and chopped it up and made a fire. The keeper of the temple came and found him doing this but he recognised this was a great Zen Abbot. He protested to him and said, 'What have you done, how, why have you desecrated, destroyed this Buddha?' The fire was by this time dying down and the Zen Master went to the ashes and he poked about with a stick for a long time. He seemed to be looking for something and the man said: 'What are you doing? What are you looking for? Too late now.' The Abbot said, 'I am looking for the *sharira.*' The Buddhist tradition is that when a perfect man is burnt, rather like the Russian belief in the Christian tradition, there are certain elements that don't get burnt which show that he is a perfect being. So he said to the man: 'I am looking for the sign of this Buddha, the *sharira.*' And the man said, 'What do you mean? This is only a wooden Buddha.' 'Then,' he said, 'can I have the other two for my fire?' The meaning is not to remain worshipping what is only a wooden Self, so to speak, what is only an unreal Self, but to penetrate the *antahkarana*, the personality, and to find the reality behind.

The worship of the Lord, the worship of Shri Krishna, of Christ or of Buddha, is the time-honoured means of escape from the tyranny of ego worship, from this bondage of ignorance, as it is called. The narrow self-interest, the interests of the ego, and the higher interests, the interests of altruism are opposed to each other and the two cannot exist together. When man's life is transformed into a continuous act of worship, into altruism, says the *Gita*, then the bondage to the narrow self-interest is lost. It means, as Swami Rama Tirtha says, giving the reins of the mind into the hands of the Lord Shri Krishna, the divine charioteer. It means taking one's stand on the highest part of the personality, on the divine part of the personality.

The *Gita* speaks of the two paths. It is possible, says the *Gita*, to try and approach the transcendental being directly but 'easier is the path of those who approach through the means of worship', through worshipping the Lord in His universal form, as the Lord of the universe, His personal form. Because, as the promise is given in the *Gita*, 'through exclusive devotion to Me, O Arjuna, I speedily deliver them from the ocean of *sansara.*'[65]

The aim of Yoga, one can say, is to get beyond the mind, is to get beyond the images of the mind to the reality behind. But this is the time-honoured method by which it is done. The knowledge promised by the Yoga and by the mystics is not like knowledge of empirical science or empirical detail. We can go to science for this kind of knowledge; we can go to sense perception, we can go to libraries. But the aim of Yoga is a knowledge of the fundamental nature of experience, of the reality behind the mind, of 'He in Whom the universe lives and moves and has its being,' and in order to get this knowledge we have to go beyond the mind. Shri Dadaji said, 'Silence is the court of God.' The approach to God is by silencing the mind. This is the way we must travel. We must be able, voluntarily, first to restrain and then to silence the mind.

Finally, I give you a short meditation practice which Dr Shastri himself gave at a lecture. If you wish to, you can put it to the test in the months ahead. The practice is first of all to breathe a few times, taking the sound OM. This is the sound corresponding to the symbol which is the highest reality in the East. Breathe a few times, saying aloud or silently this sound OM, and then take this text with the idea of steeping the mind in its meaning:

> 'OM. HE WHO IS THE SPLENDOUR OF THE SUN SHINES IN MY MIND AS MY SELF. HE IS MY "I", HE IS TRUTH, HE IS ALL. OM.'

---

[65]*Bhagavad Gita* XII, 5,6 and 7.

The meaning is: the sun is the ultimate source of all outer light. Then there is the inner light of the intellect, the light by which we see right and wrong. And then behind that there is the spiritual light which illumines even this intellect, being the light of the intellect.

These lectures are given in a spirit of service to present the truth which we received from our teacher, and at his request we are doing it.

11

The Fruits of Meditation[*]

IF ONE HAD to put in one sentence the practical case for practising Meditation-Yoga one might sum it up in the phrase: 'Unless you can control your mind, your mind will control you.' As Milton said: 'The mind is its own place and in itself can make a heaven of hell, a hell of heaven.'

Therefore, one of the cardinal principles of Yoga is the active use of the mind and not the passive suffering of the mind. Man must live consciously. All too often in life we find ourselves at the mercy not only of outer circumstances, but of the inner states of our mind as well. The ordinary man is often the victim of the moods and irrational impulses of his own mind, rather than the master of an instrument which can bring him great peace, happiness and wisdom. So long as we are at the mercy of unthinking prejudices, blind superstitions and uncritically accepted dogmas – not only religious dogmas, but political dogmas, social dogmas and economic dogmas – we cannot be called free men. Only that man who is open to receive truth from wherever it comes can be called free, who has, as we say, an open mind, not a closed mind. It is for this reason that Yoga claims to be a means to liberate man's spirit and it is as well to remember that this claim is shared with other great spiritual traditions. 'Know ye the truth and the truth shall make you free,'[66]

---

[*]A lecture given on 19th October 1968.

[66]Gospel John VIII, 32.

was the teaching of Jesus. When the people asked him what he could possibly mean by such an extraordinary statement because they had never been in slavery to anyone, he replied quite simply that every man was a bondslave to the lower urges of his own mind. If the lower propensities of the mind are not controlled and transformed into a fund of useful and creative energy, then the mind is a great enemy of man. Therefore, the principle of Yoga is active use of the mind, not passive suffering of the mind. This is the purpose of the practice of mind control and meditation.

In the Eastern classics, this process is often likened to the breaking in and training of a wild horse or an ox. The mind is, in its raw state, unpredictable and untamed and, like an unbroken colt, it will shy from any attempts to apply the rein and the harness, but like the horse and the ox, it is potentially a great ally of man, able to carry him as a rider to where he wants to go and able to work for him. The conscious direction of the mind, which is the Yoga training, is like the breaking in and training of the horse, and there are various stages in the process. First, it must be possible to control the mind and to make it stand still under the rider's direction. It is no good having a mind which is dashing off wildly and uncontrollably in this direction and that, overcome at one moment by a mood of despair, at the next anxious and fearful, at the next subject to an outburst of anger. Such a mind is a menace both to its owner and to those around.

The first necessity in training the mind is to achieve mental relaxation. This may sound like a paradox and some people may suppose that Yoga practice aims at rendering the mind inactive and useless, fit for nothing but gazing into empty space, but this is a complete misunderstanding of the Yoga training. The first aim is to achieve active relaxation, not passive relaxation. Throughout life, the mind is subject to passive contraction and overactivity. Tension and worry, great curses of the uncontrolled mind, are a kind of chronic mental spasm or contraction in which the individual is not an active agent, but a passive victim. Therefore, we have to offset this passive contraction of the mind by active relaxation of the mind.

Why active relaxation? Because there must be effort initially, effort to acquire the stilling of the overactive mind. It is like the efforts of the rider to capture the untamed horse and get it to stand still so that he can mount it and begin the second stage of the training.

Many of the initial practices of Yoga, which you will find described in our founder Dr Shastri's book on meditation, are simply aimed at achieving this active relaxation of the mind. A great aid can be to take a number of deep breaths, to control the breathing consciously and to retain each breath about twice as long as it takes to take it in fully. By concentrating on breathing consciously in this way, the mind can be pacified as a preliminary to meditation. It is a powerful means of relaxing the tension of the nerves. After the mind is stilled, it then has to be concentrated and focussed on to a point. This again implies restraint of the activity of the mind, but this focussed inactivity is not inaction but the height of creative mental activity.

As another illustration, a cat crouched and focussed, ready to spring, may be perfectly motionless and is certainly an example of one-pointed concentration, but it is not an inactive cat; it is a cat achieving a rare moment of concentrated mental activity. To superficial inspection it may be even more motionless than a cat lying asleep and breathing gently after lapping up a bowl of milk, but the greater motionlessness of the crouched cat is really intense activity. So with the still and concentrated mind. It may appear to be a state of inaction but it is really the height of mental activity.

The *Bhagavad Gita* chapter four, verse eighteen teaches: 'He who can see inaction in action, who can also see action in inaction, he is wise among men...'[67] Most mental activity is aimless and fruitless, it is action which amounts to inaction because it is pointless. By stopping the mind's activity and controlling it, it can be rendered creative. This restraint of activity, this inactivity, is the highest activity.

When you see an eye surgeon operating or a watchmaker at work, their movements may be very small, certainly much smaller than those of a navvy or a tick-tack bookmaker, transmitting the odds to his colleague on the racecourse, but their activity is more creative. The characteristics of that activity are that there is intense concentration and that from their skill, derived from long practice, there is confidence and economy in that activity, and there is no unnecessary effort or overactivity. A mind which is always jumping about, a dithering mind or even a so-called brilliant mind, which is always throwing off a dazzling display of mental acrobatics or fireworks, is not the most creative mind.

Some years ago there was an interview on the radio, of a man who had had an astonishing success in training horses. He was asked what the secret of his success was and he said that the first thing in training a horse was to get it to stand still. He said that if you could get a horse to the point that it would stand still and you could stand in front of it and breathe up its nostrils, you would thereafter be able to do absolutely anything with it, because you would have completely gained its confidence.

---

[67] *Bhagavad Gita* IV. 18.

I am not competent to say whether this is true about horses, but it is not a bad illustration of how the Yogis say one should gain control of the mind. When you can get it to stand completely still and watch the breathing, you will achieve control over its functions which will remain at other times in active life as well. The trouble is that our minds are a battlefield of discordant desires and urges and getting it to stand still is not as easy as it sounds. Sometimes it seems more like a tiger than a horse and restraining it can be a formidable process. This is well enough recognised by the Yogis. The pupil Arjuna complains to the teacher Shri Krishna in the *Gita* that his mind is restless, turbulent, strong and obstinate, and that it seems as difficult to control it as to control the wind (Chapter VI, verse 34). The teacher replies that it is undoubtedly restless and difficult to restrain, but by the practice of Yoga it can be controlled by the proper means.

It should be clear to you that the first of the fruits of meditation is that it enables the individual to escape from suffering the vagaries and moods of the uncontrolled mind. It enables him to free himself from the pointless and unproductive inner tension of the uncontrolled mind and thus to release the creative energies of the mind for use in consciously directed activity. When one is able to use the mind at will, then the mental activities can be made creative instead of destructive and there is also a great bonus in the form of inner peace and equanimity which cannot be disturbed even by difficult circumstances.

The following is an illustration of the attitude of the Eastern teachers to the problem of dealing with the mind, and the way in which they teach their pupils. A man, who was having a very difficult life because of the uncontrolled outbursts of anger to which he was liable, went for advice to a spiritual teacher and told him of his difficulty. He said: 'I have an uncontrollable temper and it is making my life hell. Can you help me to cure it?' The teacher replied: 'You have something very interesting. Let me see it. Just produce it for me now.' The man responded: 'But I can't. It comes over me suddenly and I never know when it is coming!' The teacher said: 'Well, if you can't produce it and it comes over you from somewhere else, it can't be your own nature.' Then he gave the man instructions in meditation practice and how to control the mind. This illustrates the fact that it is our attitude of passively suffering the mind, rather than actively controlling it, which is at fault. The first principle of Yoga training is to take charge of the mind and train it, as a rider breaks in a horse.

In the Chinese classics, where the mind is symbolised as an ox rather than a horse, this stage of the mind training is described in the verse:[68]

> 'I seize him with a terrific struggle.
> His great will and power are inexhaustible.
> He charges to the high plateau far above the cloud mists,
> Or stands in an impenetrable ravine.'

But this is only before the ox or the mind is first caught, when he is used to getting his own way. Then comes the stage of taming the ox, of the patient practice of mind control. On this the poet says:[69]

> 'The whip and rope are necessary,
> Else he might stray off down some dusty road.

[68] 12th century Chinese master Kakuan's paintings, verse and prose on the Buddhist path to enlightenment: *The Ten Bulls*.

[69] 12th century Chinese master Kakuan's paintings, verse and prose on the Buddhist path to enlightenment: *The Ten Bulls*.

Being well trained, he becomes naturally gentle.
Then, unfettered, he obeys his master.'

Controlling the mind does not mean fighting it. The best trainers are not aggressive and domineering, nor do they use cruelty. The training is a function of applying wisdom and willpower. To another seeker who came complaining of the undesirable thoughts and images which filled his mind, our own teacher's teacher gave the instruction simply to sit still and concentrate on stilling the mind, without trying to struggle with it, to repeatedly bring it back to concentrate on the breathing practice or the text of the meditation each time it was found to have strayed. He gave the illustration of a glass of muddy water. The best way to clear it, is not to disturb it but to leave it as still as possible so that the dust particles settle to the bottom. This stilling of the mind voluntarily not only brings control of the mind, it also leads to the tranquillisation and purification of the mind.

However, breaking in and mounting the steed of the mind is only the first stage. It must then be trained, remaining still in the paddock, before there can be any question of letting it out on the open road so that it can take you where you want to go. The restraint and stilling of the mind is a prelude to concentration and enquiry. This further stage is called by the Indian Yogis the practice of enquiry (*vichara*) which leads to Self-knowledge, and by the Chinese sages more poetically, 'slowly riding the ox home'. The *Upanishads* do, in fact, use somewhat the same simile as the Chinese when they speak of the ordinary man as like someone who has been blindfolded by bandits and left far from his home in the middle of the forest. He has to remove the blindfold and then by setting out on a search, asking the way from place to place as he goes, to find his way home.

Why is man not at home already? What has he got to seek further anyway? Does he not know perfectly well who he is here and now? It is not only the Yogis who tell man that he does not know who he is. Schrödinger, one of the greatest of modern physicists, has said that the real aim of science is to answer for man the command of the Delphic oracle: 'Know thyself'. The spiritual teachers agree but part company from the scientist and the empiricist because they insist that full Self-knowledge cannot come through sense experience alone, no matter how refined and subtle the analysis of the data of sense experience is made. One of the recorded sayings of Jesus is: 'The kingdom of heaven is within you and he who knows himself shall find it'. The spiritual teachers of all the great traditions tell man that when he has tamed and mounted the horse of his mind then his real task begins. Then he has to make his journey home in order to discover who the rider really is. Who is this Self which has set out to catch the horse of the mind and then to tame it? There is an element in man above and behind the mind and it is the unchanging element which reveals itself to him through his self-consciousness, not the empirical ego, but the real I, the real Self.

The *Bhagavad Gita* (Chapter III, verses 42-43) teaches:

> 'They say that (compared with the physical body) the senses are superior; superior to the senses is the lower mind (*manas*, the impulsive nature of emotions and desires, errors and doubts); superior to the lower mind is intellect (the organ of reason and will); one who is even superior to intellect is He (the real Self, the Dweller in the body). Thus knowing Him who is superior to intellect, subduing the (lower) self

> by the (higher) Self, destroy the lower nature, hard to conquer, which is destructive of knowledge and wisdom.'

Man has a dual nature. His body and mind are the products of matter in its gross or subtle form and this, as modern physics has taught us, is itself the product of the play of electromagnetic force. It is the world of becoming of which the mystics speak. But we have still to ask, what is that ground of being, upon which these time-spatial events occur? What is the absolute ground against which the world of relativity passes by? What is the real Self in the mind which gives unity and identity to all the passing states of experience? It is to discover the answer to these questions that Yoga is to be practised. Its greatest fruit is claimed to be the achievement of full Self-knowledge. I end with two verses from the *Gita* (Chapter V, verses 16-17):

> 'For those whose unwisdom is destroyed by the wisdom of the Self, Wisdom, like the sun, illuminates that Supreme (Truth).'

> [They return home] 'their sins shaken off by means of wisdom.'

12

The God-Intoxicated Man*

ON SUNDAY, 20th February, in The Hague in Holland, a middle-aged man died while his landlord and landlady were out at church. Their lodger was a poor man who had made his living as a lens grinder. He was of Spanish or perhaps Portuguese descent and he was Jewish. A man of medium height, with fine features, rather dark-skinned, with dark curly hair and long black eyebrows. His name had originally been the Jewish, *Baruch*, but he had changed it to the equivalent, Benedict. He had been suffering for some years from tuberculosis. The event on Sunday, 20th February, did not take place thirteen days ago but exactly three hundred years earlier in 1677. The man's surname was Spinoza.

He was what would nowadays be called a dissident. And even in that tolerant country of Holland he had been made to suffer for his opinions. He was himself the most non-violent and peaceable man it would be possible to imagine – in no sense a revolutionary – but to hear what people said about him you would have thought that he was the Devil incarnate. Bertrand Russell has put it very well, describing him as the noblest and most lovable of all the great philosophers:[70]

---

*A lecture given on 4th March 1977.

[70]Bertrand Russell, *History of Western Philosophy*, 1946, p. 592.

> 'Intellectually, some others have surpassed him but ethically he is supreme. As a natural consequence, he was considered during his lifetime and for a century after his death, a man of appalling wickedness. He was born a Jew, but the Jews excommunicated him. Christians abhorred him equally; although his whole philosophy is dominated by the idea of God, the orthodox accused him of atheism. Leibniz, who owed much to him, concealed his debt, and carefully abstained from saying a word in his praise; he even went so far as to lie about the extent of his personal acquaintance with the heretic Jew.'

Spinoza had started life as the son of a successful Jewish merchant, whose forbears had emigrated to Holland from Spain to escape the persecution there. He was very early recognised as a brilliant scholar, and he showed no interest in his father's business as a merchant, preferring to spend his time in and around the synagogue, studying the Jewish classics. He was, in his teens, expected to prove a brilliant leader and teacher of the Jewish community in which he grew up. But he had also read widely among the Christian thinkers and the leading figures of the Renaissance, like Bruno and others. He was caught up in that great scientific movement of the seventeenth century which, taking its inspiration from some earlier thinkers like Leonardo and Galileo, began to try and understand the world in terms of scientific laws and mathematics.

As a result of his speculations and opinions, at the age of twenty-four Spinoza was summoned before the elders of the synagogue on a charge of heresy. He had dared to suggest that the world of nature was not simply a creation but actually a direct manifestation of God, of the Divine

Nature. He held, in other words, in direct contradiction to the teachings of the Bible, that God was immanent in every part of His Creation, and not a transcendent Being standing aloof from the world.

The elders of the synagogue were not only worried about his Jewish orthodoxy – they were perhaps legitimately concerned about the reaction of the Protestant Netherlanders who provided them with such a welcome refuge from the Catholic persecution in Spain – but they were also worried about his opinions being a challenge to the Biblical teaching, and that this might also upset the Christian authorities. In fact, when he was called before them, they offered Spinoza quite a large sum of money, to be paid yearly, if he would keep his mouth shut and consent to give, at least, lip-service to the orthodox teaching of the Jewish faith. He refused and he was excommunicated on 27th July 1656. A solemn ceremony was held in which the curses of God were called down on his head and all were admonished that none should hold converse with him by word of mouth, nor communication with him by writing; that no one should do him any service of any kind or abide under the same roof with him; or that no one should approach within four cubits length of him, nor read any document dictated by him or written by his hand.

After this his father would have nothing more to do with him and he was literally an outcast from his own community. He took it all with great dignity and courage, saying simply: 'It compels me to nothing which I should not have done in any case.' And when subsequently his sister tried to cheat him of a small inheritance, he contested the case in court, and won the case because he was in the right, and then turned over the inheritance to the sister. Shortly after his excommunication – and nobility is not without cost, remember – an attempt was made on his life as he was walking through the streets one night in Amsterdam and he narrowly escaped with a wound on his neck. After this he moved out of the city to lodge with a kindly Christian couple who lived some miles out. He managed to make a living, first of all by teaching children in a school run by a free-thinking friend of his who still remained loyal, and later by polishing lenses.

When the Christian couple moved later to Leiden, Spinoza moved with them and he lived the rest of his life with them. He lived very frugally, believing that one should not have more than is necessary to provide for one's essential needs. When, in later life, a rich merchant of Amsterdam, Simon de Prees, who became a great admirer of his, wanted to give him a large sum of money, Spinoza refused. The merchant, when he was making his will, then wanted to leave all his fortune to Spinoza, but Spinoza himself persuaded him to leave it to his brother instead. He was offered a large pension when his fame was beginning to be known late in his life by Louis XIV, on condition needless to say – and this is typical of the gifts of kings – that he dedicated his next book to the king. Well, this also he refused. He said that Nature is satisfied with little, and if she is, I am also.

Spinoza used to tell his landlord that he was like the serpent, in a circle with its tail in its mouth, because at the year's end he had nothing left. He just did enough lens-grinding to support himself. He was very careful in keeping his accounts – just enough to support himself, but not more than that because he spent any time he could on philosophy. He wrote three-and-a-half books, now recognised as classics, but the greatest of these, *Ethics*, was not published in his lifetime because the opposition of the theologians made it dangerous to publish. He tried to get it published, going to Amsterdam, but we know from a letter he wrote in 1675 to Oldenburg, a friend in England who was Secretary of the Royal Society, that he was not able to get it published. He says in that letter:[71]

> 'A rumour was spread about that a book of mine was soon to appear, in which I endeavour to prove that there is no God. This report, I regret to add, was by many received as true. Certain theologians, who probably were themselves the author of the rumour, took occasion upon this to lodge a complaint against me with the Prince and the Magistrates. Having received a hint of this state of things from trustworthy friends, who assured me further that the theologians were everywhere lying in wait for me, I determined to put off my attempted publication until such time as I should see what turn affairs should take.'

As we have said, he did not manage to publish *Ethics* in his lifetime, yet he did by the end of his life number among his friends and admirers men like Christiaan Huygens, one of the great Dutch scientists of the time, an associate of Newton in the controversy over the wave theory of light. He did receive offers, for instance, of a Chair in Philosophy from the University of Heidelberg at the end of his life, which again he said he did not want to take, although he was grateful for the offer, because he wanted freedom to think and write.

His influence after his death grew ever greater – first with thinkers like Lessing and Herder in Germany. In

[71]Benedict de Spinoza, *Correspondence*, 1886 (Reply to a letter from Oldenburg dated 22 July 1675).

Lessing's play *Nathan der Weise*, it is said that the character of the noble Jew in that work owes a lot, both to the character of Spinoza and to Moses Mendelssohn who was Lessing's other great friend. Goethe acknowledged himself a lifelong pupil and follower of Spinoza and in England in subsequent years Coleridge, Wordsworth and Shelley were much influenced by him, as later was George Eliot – but, of course, all that was a century later.

Why did Spinoza's thought provoke so much opposition in his own day? Only two of his books were published in his lifetime, but we can get an idea from some of the things that he says in the first book, which was called *Tractatus Theologico-Politicus*. In it he holds that the statements in the Bible are not to be taken literally, but are written in metaphorical or allegorical language. According to him, the contents of Scripture are necessarily adapted as far as possible to the understanding of the masses. They explain things in a way that has most power to move men, especially uneducated men, to devotion. The object is not to convince the reason, but to attract and lay hold of the imagination. He writes:[72]

> 'The masses think that the power and providence of God are most clearly displayed by any events that are extraordinary and contrary to the conception which they have formed of Nature. They suppose, indeed, that God is inactive as long as Nature works in her accustomed order. And vice versa, that the power of Nature and natural causes are idle so long as God is acting. Thus they imagine two powers distinct from one another – the power of God and the power of Nature.'

---

[72]Benedict de Spinoza, *A Theologico-Political Treatise*, 1883, ch. IV.

Spinoza held, on the contrary, that the Laws of Nature were the operation of the laws of God, and that Nature was simply a manifestation of God. Many people have as a consequence said that he was a pantheist. It has been claimed that he thought that objective Nature, as it is, was God. But he's at pains himself to reject this. He distinguishes very carefully between the creation of Nature, and the Force which creates and rules Nature. The Latin words that he uses are '*Natura naturans*' and '*Natura naturata*'. God is immanent in the whole world manifesting as the creative Force of Nature, but He is not identical to the creation, according to Spinoza. And in this view, I think, one is at once reminded of the verses in the *Bhagavad Gita*:

> 'This world made up of the elements and the mind is the inferior prakriti, or nature, but as distinct from this know thou My superior *Prakriti*, the very Life, O Mighty-Armed, by which this universe is upheld. (Chapter VII, verse 5)
>
> 'Know that all beings have their birth in these; so I am the Source and Dissolution of the whole Universe. (Chapter VII, verse 6)

And again in chapter nine:

> 'By Me all this World is pervaded, My Form unmanifested. All beings dwell in Me and I do not dwell in them.' (Chapter IX, verse 4)

These views in the *Gita* are very close, one might say, to Spinoza's. Spinoza is quite specific about his view that God is immanent in His Creation. He says:[73]

---

[73]Benedict de Spinoza, *On the Improvement of the Understanding (Treatise on the Emendation of the Intellect).*

> 'I take a totally different view of God and Nature from that which the later Christians usually entertain. For I hold that God is immanent and not the extraneous cause of all things. I say all is in God; all lives and moves in God. And this I maintain with the Apostle Paul, and perhaps with every one of the philosophers of antiquity, although in a way other than theirs. I might even venture to say that my view is the same as that entertained by the Hebrews of old, if so much may be inferred from certain traditions, greatly altered or falsified though they be. It is, however, a complete mistake on the part of those who say that my purpose is to show that God and Nature, under which last term they understand a certain mass of corporeal matter, are one and the same. I had no such intention.'

In this passage, Spinoza refers to something which we know to be true, namely, that he had studied the early Jewish mystics and a lot of the ancient mystical writers. There are references to them in his writings. The universe with all its laws is an expression, for Spinoza, of the Infinite Nature of God. Therefore, the Will of God and the Laws of Nature are one and the same Reality described in different terms. Spinoza, like the Mohammedan Sufis, is a determinist. He believes that both the operation of the mind in the individual, and the operation of the Law in Nature are fixed – not by an arbitrary decree of God, but by the very Nature of God, and that the events that take place are simply the working out of these Laws. For him, the problem of evil arises simply from our limited vision, and God is beyond the little conceptions of good and evil of the individual. He says:[74]

---

[74]Benedict de Spinoza, *On the Improvement of the Intellect.*

> 'Whenever, then, anything in Nature seems to us ridiculous, absurd or evil, it is because we have a partial knowledge of things, and are in the main ignorant of the order and coherence of Nature as a whole. And because we want everything to be arranged according to the dictates of our own reason; although, in fact, what our reason pronounces bad, is not bad as regards the order and laws of universal nature, but only as regards the laws of our own nature taken separately.'

In other words our ideas of good and evil, of beautiful and ugly, are often dictated by self-interest. Nature as we see it, then, is not identical to God according to Spinoza. God is the transcendent, infinite substratum of the world. He is the true substance in the literal sense of that word – that which stands behind Nature. The finite modes of Nature are an unreal aspect of His being. Spinoza speaks of these 'finite modes', emphasising that they have no existence independent of God. It is again like the teaching in the Vedanta philosophy. 'All beings dwell in Me,' says the Lord in the *Gita*, 'I do not dwell in them.'[75] God is infinite and cannot be contained in the finite. But the finite only lives, moves and has its being in Him – in the infinite.

Spinoza sees matter and mind as two aspects of one and the same world. Every object, he thinks, has a material aspect occupying a place in space – having the property of extension in other words – and at the same time it has a distinct mental aspect in the realm of thought. Unlike Descartes, philosophising just before Spinoza's time, he does not separate body and mind into two distinct and different realities. And so there is not the problem for him

---

[75] *Bhagavad Gita* IX, 4.

that there was for Descartes and his followers, of how the two interacted. For him they are simply two aspects of one and the same reality. In some ways one might say that Spinoza's relationship to Descartes, was rather like the relationship of the non-dualist philosophy of Vedanta to the dualistic Sankhya philosophy. Descartes had believed that there were these two distinct realities created by God, namely matter and mind. He was a dualist. But Spinoza, although he accepted something of the philosophy of Descartes and was greatly influenced by it, was a non-dualist. To him both matter and mind were partial aspects of the same reality, and neither of them were distinct from the infinite reality, God, in Whom they lived, moved and had their being. The individual, for him, was merely an aspect of the divine reality. And again one is reminded of the great texts in the Advaita classics, like the passage in the thirteenth chapter of the *Gita*, for instance:

> 'With hands and feet everywhere; with eyes, and heads and mouths everywhere; with hearing everywhere – that Reality exists enveloping all. Shining by the functions of all the senses, yet without the senses; unattached yet supporting all; devoid of qualities, yet enjoying qualities; without and within all beings; the unmoving as also the moving. Because subtle, That is incomprehensible, and near and far away is That. The Light even of lights, That is said to be beyond darkness. Knowledge, the Knowable, and the Goal of Knowledge – it is implanted in the heart of everyone.' (Chapter XIII, verses 13-17)

Perhaps we might do a little meditation on that verse from the *Gita*:

> 'OM. THE LIGHT EVEN OF LIGHTS, THAT IS SAID TO BE BEYOND DARKNESS. KNOWLEDGE, THE KNOWABLE, AND THE GOAL OF KNOWLEDGE – IT IS IMPLANTED IN THE HEART OF EVERYONE. OM'[76]

For Spinoza, no finite being is self-subsistent; every creature is a limited aspect of the infinite. One of his great sayings in fact is: 'All determination is negation.' It sounds a difficult phrase, but what he is saying really, is that in trying to define anything finite you have to do it by saying what it is not – by settling its boundaries and limits. It is much more difficult, of course, to say what it is. The real substance of the world, the reality behind the universe, must be That which has no external cause for its existence, says Spinoza. It must be self-subsistent, unlike creatures who have the reason for their existence outside themselves. And he argues that there is only one substance, infinite and eternal, and that this substance is God.

The divine nature excludes all imperfection and involves absolute perfection. If it were finite it would be limited, but there cannot be two infinite substances. Reality must be indivisible, unique and eternal. Hence, whatever is, is in God, and nothing can exist or be conceived without Him. God does not interfere with the world from outside because He is already immanent in it. He is its Inner Ruler. In fact, Spinoza would have no difficulty in accepting the verse in the eighteenth chapter of the *Gita*, which says: 'The Lord dwells in the hearts of all beings, O Arjuna, causing them to turn round by His Power of Maya as if they were mounted on a machine.'[77] Or that other verse in the ninth

---

[76] *Bhagavad Gita* XIII, 17.
[77] *Bhagavad Gita* XVIII, 61.

chapter: 'By Me presiding, Prakriti, or Nature, produces the moving and the unmoving, because of this, O Son of Kunti, the world revolves.'[78]

One of Spinoza's small books is entitled *On the Improvement of the Intellect* and in it he gives some practical advice on how to live. He tells us at the outset why he himself gave up everything to follow philosophy:[79]

> 'After experience had taught me that all things which frequently take place in ordinary life are vain and futile, and when I saw that all the things I feared and which feared me, had nothing good or bad in them save in so far as the mind was affected by them, I determined at last to enquire whether there was anything which might be truly good and able to communicate its goodness. And by which the mind might be affected to the exclusion of all other things. I determined, I say, to enquire whether I might discover, and attain the faculty of enjoying throughout eternity continual supreme happiness. I could see the many advantages acquired from honour and riches. And that I should be debarred from acquiring these things if I wished seriously to investigate a new matter. But the more one possesses either of them, the more the pleasure is increased, and the more one is in consequence encouraged to increase them. Whereas if at any time our hope is frustrated there arises in us the deepest pain. Fame has also this great drawback: that if we pursue it we must direct our lives in such a way as to please the fancy of men, avoiding what they dislike and

---

[78]*Bhagavad Gita* IX, 10.

[79]Benedict de Spinoza, *On the Improvement of the Intellect.*

> seeking what pleases them. But the love towards a thing eternal and infinite alone, feeds the mind with a pleasure secure from all pain. The greatest good is the knowledge of the union which the mind has with the whole of Nature. The more the mind knows, the better it understands its forces and the order of Nature. The more it understands its forces, or strength, the better it will be able to direct itself and lay down rules for itself. And the more it understands the order of Nature, the more easily will it be able to liberate itself from useless things. This is the whole method.'

And this is the method that he goes on to discuss in that book.

What then is needed? Before all things, says Spinoza, a means must be devised for improving and clarifying the intellect. He goes on to distinguish four different kinds of knowledge which the mind brings to us.

First, there is knowledge by hearsay: things which I only know because I have been told about them. A good example, for instance, is the date of my birth, or the conditions of my early infancy. I can only know these from what I have been told about them from others.

Then there is what he calls vague, or confused knowledge. It is the knowledge that we all have of most empirical things, in which the mind gets a general idea, a general impression of how things are. This knowledge, says Spinoza, is characterised by the fact that it is made up of inadequate ideas. And it is perfectly true if you think about it. Most of the knowledge that we have, most of the general ideas we have about how things are, are not entirely consistent, and they do not hang together if we examine them carefully. But we never do examine them carefully in the ordinary way and consequently, we do not often become dissatisfied with it.

Better than this knowledge, says Spinoza, is the kind of knowledge which comes through reason, because this gives us a relatively clear and unconfused understanding of things in terms of their relationships, one with another. It is not merely a question of opinion or imagination, as it so often is in the knowledge of the former kind, the confused kind. It is much more with reason; it is made up of adequate ideas – we have thought out the things properly.

But there is something better than the knowledge which comes through reason, because rational knowledge is always discursive. It moves round the object, so to speak, explaining it in terms of what it is not or in terms of its relationship with other objects. There is some more adequate knowledge than this. This higher kind of knowledge, knowledge of the third kind as Spinoza calls it, because he ignores the hearsay knowledge – he is really concerned with the three: the confused knowledge, the rational knowledge, and the third kind of knowledge – is the intuitive knowledge, intuitive in the sense that in it a thing is known as it really is and not simply by knowledge of its causal relationships. It is what we might call in modern terms roughly, knowledge by insight.

Spinoza says that in so far as the mind consists of opinion and imagination, it is not really active in thought, it is passive. Sense knowledge is inadequate and confused, and as the *Gita* says, we are driven along by it, rather as a pilotless and rudderless ship is driven along by every passing wind and current. According to Spinoza, then, the wise man will correct and refine this confused knowledge by bringing to bear his reason. It is the principle enunciated in the *Gita*: 'Let a man raise himself by himself.'[80] By the *buddhi*, the intellect in yogic terms, the *manas*, the impulsive, unthinking *manas*, can be controlled. And again we can see this rough parallel between the Vedantic teaching of the lower mind, *manas*, and the higher intellect, *buddhi*, and the two levels of which Spinoza speaks: the confused, general, inadequate knowledge corresponding to *manas*, and the rational knowledge of *buddhi*. The lower mind, *manas* in Vedantic terms, is imaginative – it is the picture-making mind; it is opinionated; it is impulsive and irrational. *Buddhi*, on the other hand, the intellect, is the faculty which examines the pros and cons of the matter, reasons things out and determines the true facts.

The third type of knowledge of which Spinoza speaks, the intuitive knowledge which he regards as the highest kind, is also spoken of by the Yogis as a faculty which can be awakened in the enlightened *buddhi*. Spinoza says of this knowledge: 'The greatest endeavour of the mind, and its greatest virtue, is to understand things by the third class of knowledge.' And he also says that this arises from the second class and not from the first. It arises not from the confused opinionated knowledge of *manas*, but from the exercise of reason, *buddhi*. Or I suppose if we translate this to Vedantic terms, we could say that discrimination, *viveka*, is the fruit of *vichara*, intellectual enquiry. And rather sweetly Spinoza adds when he is discussing this: 'The things which I have so far been able to know by this knowledge have been very few.'[81]

For Spinoza, quite explicitly, the enlargement of knowledge is an enlargement of our knowledge of God. 'The more we understand,' he says, 'the more we understand

---

[80]*Bhagavad Gita* VI, 5.

[81]Spinoza: *Treatise on the Intellect*.

God.' And again: 'The more advanced, then, everyone is in this class of knowledge, the intuitive class, the more conscious he is of himself and of God. That is, the more perfect and blessed he is.'[82]

In the third book of *Ethics*, Spinoza maintains that each and everyone has the innate knowledge of God within his own mind, but that this knowledge is obscured by the passions, which distract us and eclipse our vision of the whole. The passions arise fundamentally, he says, from the instinct, or drive, for self-preservation, which is at the very basis of the constitution of each and every created thing. The basic drive in every created thing is what he calls *conatus*, the urge for self-preservation.

We love what we think will give us pleasure and we hate what we think will give us pain. But when we have an adequate idea of what is real and positive in ourselves, namely the divine element, the urge for self-preservation, which is such a basic drive, alters its character, says Spinoza, because we realise that what is real and positive in us unites us to the whole, whereas what preserves the appearance of separateness and individuality is a false appearance. In these teachings, Spinoza gets very near indeed to the Yogic philosophy.

One is reminded, for instance, of the simile in the first chapter of *Panchadashi*, which speaks of true Self-knowledge in each and every mind being obscured by the mental obstacles, in the same way as the voice of the particular child, which the father had gone to try and hear, was drowned in the chorus of children reciting the lesson in the Indian village school. It was only when the teacher silenced the voices of the other children one by one that the father could hear the voice of his son for whom he had

---

[82]Spinoza: *Ethics*.

been listening, and whom he realised then had been saying the lesson all the time. So it is, then, with the knowledge of God, according to both Swami Vidyaranya and Spinoza. It is already there, but the obstacles, the passions, in the mind distract us and prevent us from realising it. Again in Spinoza's insistence on the fundamental drive of self-preservation, the explanation of the instincts in terms of self-interest, one is reminded so often of the twelfth chapter of *Panchadashi*, which is a commentary on the passage from the *Upanishad* which stresses: 'Not for the sake of the object is the object dear, but for the sake of the Self is the object dear.'[83]

The last two books of *Ethics* are on bondage and freedom. The first is, in fact, entitled 'Of Human Bondage or the Strength of the Emotions' and the last one 'Of the Power of the Understanding or of Human Freedom'. According to Spinoza, we are in bondage in so far as we are controlled by forces which arise outside ourselves and hold us passively in their power. Conversely, we are free in so far as we are actively in control of our destiny. The forces which impinge on us do not, of course, necessarily come from the outside world, they also arise outside ourselves, so to speak, in the mind and sweep it away out of control, as the *Gita* says, 'like the wind carrying away a ship on water.'[84] The passions are things which make us passive, says Spinoza, because we lose control when we are in their power. Wrong action or unwisdom is due to error and is the result of inadequate ideas or confused knowledge. It is almost the same doctrine as we find in the *Gita*: 'The Lord takes neither the evil nor even the good deed of any. Wisdom is enveloped by unwisdom, thereby mortals are deluded. But those whose

---

[83]A summarized version of *Brihadaranyaka Upanishad* II. iv. 5

[84]*Bhagavad Gita* II, 67.

unwisdom is destroyed by wisdom of the Self, like the sun wisdom illuminates That Supreme.'[85]

According to Spinoza, there are three fundamental passions or emotions: desire, pleasure and pain. He says that it is equally true of animals and man. We do not desire something because we think it is good, on the contrary, we call it good because we desire it. Similarly, we call evil or bad anything for which we feel aversion. And all objects are judged good or bad according to our emotions; according to the desire or aversion, or in Yogic terms the *raga* and *dwesha*, we have for them. As the twelfth chapter of *Panchadashi* maintains, what we normally associate with pleasure is something which feeds our self-interest, heightens our vitality, or our drive to self-preservation and increase of power. These are the things which we love and call good. Conversely, what threatens our instinct for self-preservation is hated and called bad.

But Spinoza adds that not all emotions are passions. Hate is never anything but a passion, but love can be. When love becomes based on a deeper understanding, on an adequate idea, if you like, or a deeper vision, it is no longer inadequate and it ceases to be a passion. Liberation in fact, says Spinoza, consists in changing passive emotions into active emotions. With a deeper understanding of self-interest, as the interest of the Higher Self which unites us with others, our feeling for self-preservation becomes less individualistic. We cannot go into this in detail now, but an example, for instance, is the mother's love for her child.

Bondage for Spinoza is the human lack of power in moderating and checking the passions. As a result, we may be constrained to do what is worse even though we recognise what is better. Again, one hears in this passage

[85]*Bhagavad Gita* V, 15 and 16.

echoes of the third chapter of the *Gita*. The great path to freedom from servitude to the passions, says Spinoza, is understanding. The life of the wise man is the life of virtue and reason, which liberates him by giving him control of his own destiny. And the highest function of the mind is to know God, for it is to see the Reality behind the world. 'The love of God,' in Spinoza's words, 'is our salvation, blessedness or liberty.' Spinoza does not believe in personal immortality, but he believes that there is an immortal element in the human mind which is eternal, and that it is this element which can be enlightened.

Finally, the closing passage from *Ethics* in which Spinoza sums up what he has tried to do:[86]

> 'Thus I have completed all I wish to show concerning the power of the mind over emotions or the freedom of the mind. From which it is clear how much a wise man is in front of, and how stronger he is than an ignorant one who is guided by lust alone. For an ignorant man, besides being agitated in many ways by external causes never enjoys one true satisfaction of the mind. He lives moreover almost unconscious of himself, God and things, and as soon as he ceases to be passive ceases to be. On the contrary, the wise man in so far as he is considered as such, is scarcely moved in spirit. He is conscious of himself, of God, and things by a certain eternal necessity. He never ceases to be and always enjoys satisfaction of the mind. If the road I have shown to lead to this is very difficult it can yet be discovered. And clearly it must be very hard when it is so seldom found. For how could it be that it is neglected practically by all if

[86]Benedict de Spinoza, *A Theologico-Political Treatise*, 1883, ch. IV.

salvation were close at hand and could be found without difficulty? But all excellent things are as difficult as they are rare.'

13

Living Yoga*

THE FOLKLORE OF every country whether Eastern or Western has certain recurrent themes which reveal a great deal about the human mind. One of these themes, which appears again and again, is the theme of some magic object which will grant man any desire he may have. Most of us in the West were brought up on the stories of Aladdin's lamp or of Merlin's wand and these magic objects have their counterparts in Indian mythology too. Indian children, for instance, were told that in the middle of Indra's heaven there was said to be a wish-fulfilling tree, Kalyana Kalpataru, which could grant those who resorted to it whatever they wanted. In another of the old classics, the *Mahabharata*, one of the Rishis is said to have had a wish-fulfilling cow called Kamadenu which again granted the desires of its possessor.

Much of man's life is coloured by a yearning sense of dissatisfaction, a feeling that the world is not as he desires it to be. In the words of Omar Khayyam: 'O Love, could thou and I with Fate conspire to grasp this sorry scheme of things entire, would we not shatter it to bits and then remould it nearer to the heart's desire?'[87] The theme which runs through the poem of Omar Khayyam runs through much of human experience, and it is that man's desires are

---

*A lecture given on 16th May 1969.

[87] *The Rubaiyat of Omar Khayyam* - quatrain 88 - 11th century

thwarted and unrealised. As the legends and fairy stories teach, it is only by supernatural means, only by some magic device, that what man desires can be realised.

Now, the teaching of Yoga which we are trying to present to you is startlingly different from this. The Yogis, in fact, warn man, and it is a warning rather than a promise, *whatever you desire you will get.* They tell man, in fact, that any desire which he conceives and cultivates is bound to be fulfilled in one way or another. Desire, the yogic psychology tells us, is a canalisation of mental energy and, by the law of cause and effect, which works inexorably on the mental plane just as it does on the physical plane, that canalisation of mental energy will inevitably produce a result. If you tell an ordinary unthinking man that whatever he desires he will get, and if he believes you, of course he will regard it as the greatest bit of good fortune that could possibly have befallen him. Again, so long as he believes you, he will regard you as his greatest benefactor for telling him so. But the wise man when he is told this, and when he comes to think about it carefully, that whatever he desires he will get, will hardly take this view. The fact is, say the Yogis, that the real wish-fulfilling tree, the real magic device which grants man his desire, is nothing other than the human mind, the human mind of the individual. When it has conceived a desire and cultivated it, then, in some form or another, we shall inevitably get what we have wanted. We may not like it, of course, when we get it, but the desires will find fructification. We are all the time, say the Yogis, sowing the seeds of the future in our own present thought and action.

Now, one can imagine people objecting to this idea, protesting that even to suggest that one's desires are fulfilled is patently untrue. A man, for instance, may have intensely desired to get two tickets for the Cup Final but have signally failed to get them. We may have desired in our younger days to go to a particular school and have failed to get in, or to attend the Olympic Games and have been prevented from doing so by economic or other circumstances. So certainly in this sense not all desires are satisfied, that is to say, immediately or in the concrete form in which we have them. But what the Yogis are saying is not this. What they are saying is that all desires represent a focussing of the creative mental energy and that they will produce their effect in the long run, and that when a man realises this about his mental life, he will adopt a far more responsible attitude as to what he desires. The desires that we harbour in our mind are indeed a binding or a liberating force in our life, for as the *Upanishad* says, they help to determine what we ourselves will become. 'As a man desires, so is he,' says the *Chandogya Upanishad.* There is an old proverb: 'If the gods offer thee a boon, think well before making thy choice'. If we once realise, say the Yogis, how potently our own desires affect our future, we should be much more careful to choose the objects of our desire wisely.

When we think about it, the fact is that we often want too little from life because we give the matter little or no thought. We are content to settle for trivial desires, aiming for nothing in particular, just little momentary satisfactions of everyday life. And in this way, say the Yogis, because we don't realise what is happening, our life gets frittered away, so to speak, passing from one insignificant desire to the next, and we sell our soul for a mess of potage.

If we look indeed at those who have lived creatively, in whatever field we take, we shall find, on the contrary, that people who have lived such lives have had what our teacher used to call a master passion, a burning and sustained desire which they cultivated with considerable one-pointedness.

Christopher Columbus, long before he set sail for the West, had for years spent much of his life dreaming of exploring in this direction, reading all the books he could find, trying to get a patron to support him in the venture, and dreaming of the possibilities of finding a route to the Spice Islands through sailing to the West.

The great German archaeologist, Heinrich Schliemann, spent fifty years of his life reading, thinking and dreaming about the ancient city of Troy and its history. His one desire, even in his teens, was to find Homer's Troy. He was a poor boy, he lost his father, he had to work in a very poor shop in the port of the north German town in which he lived, simply serving behind the counter. He gradually made enough money so that towards the end of his life he could go out and search for the city of Troy. And he succeeded. It's a wonderful story really – he succeeded not only in finding the site of the ancient city of Troy, he also succeeded in finding and excavating the Mycenaean forts from which the Greek armies had set out to attack Troy.

Both the explorer Columbus and the archaeologist Schliemann had conceived a desire, had cultivated it with great perseverance and one-pointedness for much of their life, and in this way it finally produced its effect.

If we think of the sphere of politics, a very good example is Karl Marx who had this master desire to understand the forces ruling society and to bring about the proletarian revolution. His desire too, because it was sustained, was in the end very creative; whether it was a good creation or a bad creation is another question, but it was certainly very creative and it changed the whole face of the world.

In the sphere of science and technology there are hundreds of examples. The Scots inventor Baird, for instance, spent much of his life trying to realise his desire, which only he had at that time, to make television a practical reality. And then he succeeded, with the results that we all enjoy – or not, as the case may be. The same can be seen in the life of Sir Frank Whittle who, again as an individual, and against great opposition, dreamed of making the jet a practical method of propulsion for aircraft. These were all people who conceived a desire, cultivated it and eventually realised it. They are a good example of what the Yogis mean by desire being creative. But to make such dreams effective we need more than fantasy and imagination, say the Yogis, we need also a strong will and a disciplined mind.

From our point of view, in presenting to you the teachings from the yogic angle, it follows that it is quite erroneous to imagine that the individual is powerless. On the contrary, each man has the power to realise himself in whatever way he chooses. This is not to say that a particular concrete desire of his will necessarily be realised as it is conceived here and now, but that in the mind he has a potent creative force which will help to effect and materialise whatever it is focussed on with intensity. This is a universal principle of mental life, say the Yogis, applicable to the Yogi and the non-Yogi alike. Any sensible man who realises its truth will see that it means that we should carefully examine and question our desires and that it is madness to accept them uncritically. If we don't weed out silly or mistaken desires we may find that their fructification turns out to be like the fulfilment of the witches' promises to Macbeth. We may get the letter of what we desired, of what we asked for, but it will be a bitter disappointment.

One of the Indian mystics has a verse: 'Thy soul is a book; thy deeds and thoughts are the writing in it; set down only what is fair, O brother, for the pen is in thine own hand.'

The teaching of Yoga, then, is that we must examine our desires in the light of reason and execute only those which are wise. There are three great principles one can say in the yogic practice: weeding out the foolish desires, cultivating the wise ones and then a further principle is added, not simply these two – weeding out the foolish ones and cultivating the wise ones – but something further, silencing the desires in meditation. This is the peculiar contribution of the yogic practice, the silencing of the desires in meditation. The mind, say the Yogis, is a kind of battleground of conflicting desires, and while this noisy barrage is going on all the time we cannot think straight or make wise decisions. Desires are like salesmen or confidence tricksters whose main technique is to talk fast, to get us off our guard, to get their foot in the door, so to speak, and to break down our sales resistance before we have time to consider the matter seriously. If we are like a foolish householder – I won't say housewife! – we will have been carried away and have signed the contract without reading it before we realise that we can't afford to pay the price or, at any rate, that it is a waste of money.

When desires rise in the mind, say the Yogis, they paint a rosy picture, as we all know. How lovely it would be if so-and-so were the case or if I did so-and-so. And it is only if we bring reason to bear that we realise what the cost is. It's like the salesman. He paints a wonderful picture of how the vacuum cleaner will reduce three hours' work to five minutes. He doesn't tell you anything about the need to empty it or carry the contents to the dustbin or that it goes wrong – none of this is dealt with. So a rosy picture is presented, and it is not until afterwards, when we have thought about it, that we realise there is always a cost and that we consider whether it is worth the cost. Of course, if it is something worthwhile it doesn't matter that the price is high, we shall be prepared to pay it. But unless we consider the matter carefully when the desires come up in the mind, they are accepted uncritically.

If we want something worthwhile, of course, then we must want it enough to be willing to pay, to be willing to forego some other less desirable thing in order to realise it. If we wish to realise our higher aims quickly, say the Yogis, we must have urgency and we must be prepared to pay the price. This, after all, is the only real test, not only to others but to ourselves as well, of how much we truly want something. The mystic, Rumi, says that the gold of aspiration is tested in the fire of adversity. If it isn't really gold, if it's only a counterfeit alloy, if it's only something we think we want but we don't really want, then when we are asked to pay the price, it won't come through that fire, that test, unchanged.

Anything worthwhile demands sacrifice. When the great Johann Sebastian Bach was a young man between his nineteenth and his thirty-fifth year, he was mad to master everything that was known about organ playing. This period of Bach's life is the period where he was primarily an organist, a player on the organ, and it was only later that he produced his great choral music. At this period of his life he wanted to know everything there was to know about the organ. He was relatively poor but he knew that one of the greatest organists, Johann Adam Reinken, lived in Hamburg and Reinken was already a very old man but he was recognised as a master.

Bach walked on foot hundreds of miles in order to hear him playing the organ, not once but five times. Reinken didn't die until he was ninety-nine, he was really very much senior to Bach, from the century before. On the last occasion when he went to Reinken, Bach was allowed to play to Reinken and

Reinken heard him improvising for the first time on a chorale. The old man said: 'I thought that this art was dead but now I find that it lives on in you.' Well, this willingness of Bach's to walk many hundreds of miles in order to learn what he had set his heart on, his desire to master organ playing, is a good example of creative desire. One of the stories that is told is that, on one of these occasions, when he was walking home having exhausted the little money he had saved, he stopped at an inn and he was given a fish to eat. In the fish he found two gold coins and he at once turned back, went back to Hamburg, had another day or two with Reinken and then came home.

In the yogic tradition, there is the story about Shri Shuka. When Shri Shuka went for spiritual teaching to the god of death, Yama, his desire for the teaching was tested by Yama, first of all by keeping him waiting for some days and then by offering to satisfy other inferior desires. He wanted to find out whether he really wanted knowledge. He offered him riches, he offered him pleasure, or good food, because he wanted to know if Shuka had really qualified himself for the teaching. And you know, in the story he refused these other things and said, 'No, I come in order to learn. Please teach me.'

Therefore, Yoga means educating and refining our emotions. Our feelings, our desires are undisciplined and undirected. If we are to have wisdom, say the Yogis, if our feelings are to help us to live well, we must control them and consciously direct them. Even Bertrand Russell makes the point that there is a great difference between wisdom and intelligence. He says the real difference between wisdom and intelligence lies in feeling. Wisdom isn't the development of a razor sharp intellect. It lies in the education and refinement of the feelings, of the emotions. When the feelings are truly refined, one might say when they are truly human, then a man can be called wise.

From the biological point of view, man's evolution from his animal ancestors is the history of the emergence of reason on the one hand, and on the other hand of the gradual civilisation of the conflict of the raw and untamed animal emotions. The taming of the blind instincts of hate, jealousy, acquisitiveness and selfishness, and the gradual harmonisation of the personality – this is what truly makes man man. One of the characters which our teacher laid great stress on in the yogic training was the character of human-heartedness, of truly human feelings.

Just as a wise man does not sign an unread and unconsidered contract, particularly while he is under high pressure sales talk from a promoter, but says, 'No, I understand, I have heard what you have said but I want to take this contract away; I am not going to be rushed into anything. I will take the document, and I will think about it quietly and I will let you know', so, say the Yogis, the wise man will learn to still the mind and to quieten the babble of desires and impressions by practising daily a period of meditation. When he can stand back from the mind, when he can leave the desires and then come back and consider them objectively in a proper perspective, then he has wisdom. Even when the mental salesman returns he will be prepared for him, and this, say the Yogis, is the way to make the right decisions in life.

Of course, this is not the whole of Yoga, nor even the whole of dealing with the mind in everyday life. It is just as disastrous to be prevented from executing a worthwhile scheme as it is to be steamrollered into a worthless one. Here again, say the Yogis, the man who can still and control his mind will be at a real advantage.

Whenever one decides to do something worthwhile it usually involves the prospect of a sustained effort over a considerable period of time. But soon, inevitably, many distractions and counter-pulls arise. They are like settling down at home to do some work and then the doorbell rings and the stream of unwanted salesmen follow each other one after the other; one has to refuse to answer the door or send them away. There are also many, very insistent, mental distractions of the same kind.

There are also the false friends whom you will find very willing to talk about your scheme, but when it comes to actually doing something about it, it's a different matter. As a student, one well remembers that there were some students who were always to be found talking in the coffee bar of the Students' Union. Whatever time you happened to go in there, morning, noon or night, they were in the same group, often at the same table with an array of empty coffee cups and full ashtrays surrounding them. Others came and went and enjoyed their company often for fifteen or thirty minutes, but they remained. Needless to say, their names did not appear on the list of successful examination candidates at the end of term. They found at the end that they had done nothing. They had simply remained, in the poet's phrase, chewing the cud of sweet and bitter fancy while the rest of the world was getting on with doing things. One may say, well, it's an existence more worthy of a cow than a man, this chewing the cud. But then at least the cow produces milk.

Even activity, of course, can be an excuse for not doing something constructive. One can say, although this is only one aspect of things, that much of the political agitation and demonstrating has become a kind of social displacement activity, as the psychologists say, preventing people from getting on and doing something really creative. Experimental psychologists who studied animals a great deal found that if you give an animal something which it doesn't particularly like doing, or if you give it a task which is a little bit too hard for it, you may find it suddenly turning away from the task in hand and energetically scratching itself or looking interested in the other direction, or exploring with great enthusiasm some other part of the room. This is called displacement activity. It is a very good excuse for not getting on with what you ought to be doing.

Well, there is no question that an analogous process goes on in human affairs. We have a good deal of displacement activity going on. It is essentially uncreative because it aims at nothing positive and it simply wastes time and energy and disrupts society. So, say the Yogis, if we want to make efforts, even efforts in reform or efforts in the social sphere, then they should be creative, they should be decided wisely.

The life that Yoga advocates is a life of active and conscious direction of the mind. Yoga is a living thing and it is concerned with living. We have to make these teachings alive in ourselves. It is only in the living mind that Yoga can be practised, not as a theory but as a growing and developing state of mind which will bear fruit in daily life and in the opening out of the personality. It is like gardening. You cannot practise gardening simply by reading books or looking at pictures, or by going from case to case in a museum. It is easy to arrange a series of dried specimens, of course, to show every stage of growth; the seed, the germinating seedling, the young shoots, the sprouting plants, the flowering plant and the fruit. Descriptions of the stages of Yoga are like the descriptions of the different stages of plant growth. But even to put in one seed of your own and to see it sprouting will teach you more and give you more satisfaction than spending months in the Royal Horticultural Society's library, because the process will at once have become alive and interesting and practical in your own experience. What matters to us ultimately is experience, what we actually see happening before our own inner eyes. Swami Rama Tirtha used to say that discussions on Vedanta in the drawing-room are like paper flowers compared with real flowers. They may have the form of the flower but they have none of the fragrance.

Finally, since the point that is being made is that Yoga is nothing if it is not a practical thing, I offer you an outline of a scheme of practical suggestions which Dr Shastri gave in order to enable a newcomer to Yoga to obtain control of his mind and his will. There are four separate points in this programme.

The first practice is to live according to a plan. In the morning, before starting the day's work, sit in a comfortable yet controlled posture on the floor or, if necessary, on a chair. Shut your eyes and tell yourself that you will not open them for ten minutes. Then in a mood of reverence and relaxation, for tension is the enemy of life, silently repeat a name of God – OM, Jesus or any other name that appeals to you – this is the first practice.

The second practice is to take a spiritual classic and say: 'I will read a few verses over fifteen times, thinking on their meaning, and whatever happens, I will not listen to my mind if it wishes to wander.'

Finally, there are two more short practices to complete the series. The third is to send out rays of love from your heart to cover the whole world. If you cannot imagine this, say: 'My heart is radiating love which is filling the whole world.'

The fourth practice Dr Shastri gave is to forgive anyone against whom you may have what is called a reasonable grievance.

This lecture has been a commentary on a passage from Dr Shastri's biography of his teacher, *The Heart of the Eastern Mystical Teaching*. In chapter twenty-five his teacher Shri Dada is speaking to his pupils:

> 'Please think of the following illustration. The Lord has provided us with ground and with seed and has given us a knowledge of the seasons at which the seed ought to be sown and also a knowledge of weeding, watering, manuring and pruning. Now if a peasant passes the time of sowing in gossiping, smoking and sleeping and neglects to sow the seeds until the monsoon has set in, or fails to look after the young crop, he will naturally lose both seed and harvest. And who is to blame? Every jiva, every soul, is free to act in one of various ways open to him and his present state is the direct outcome of his past choices. He has therefore every chance to better his present actions and to improve his future state. Happiness and worldly success are two different things. The latter is a phantom, a baseless show, a bubble. But happiness is the more satisfying result of the application of dharma, of righteousness.'[88]

---

[88]Hari Prasad Shastri, *The Heart of the Eastern Mystical Teaching*, Shanti Sadan.

REFERENCES

The lectures reproduced here were given between 1961 and 1977. References have been gleaned from notes in the margins of the lecturer's original draft, books owned by the lecturer and internet searches. Many of the longer quotations are from documents that are recognised spiritual sources, out of copyright or are in the public domain. The compilers would like to thank the Cambridge University Press and Harper and Collins who have given their permission to quote from their publications. There are a few instances where the source of original quotes has not been established and the compilers hope that those who own the copyright will let us know so that we can put the record straight in future editions.